Listen to the Butterflies!
Valuable Life Lessons Learned from Some Amazing Creatures

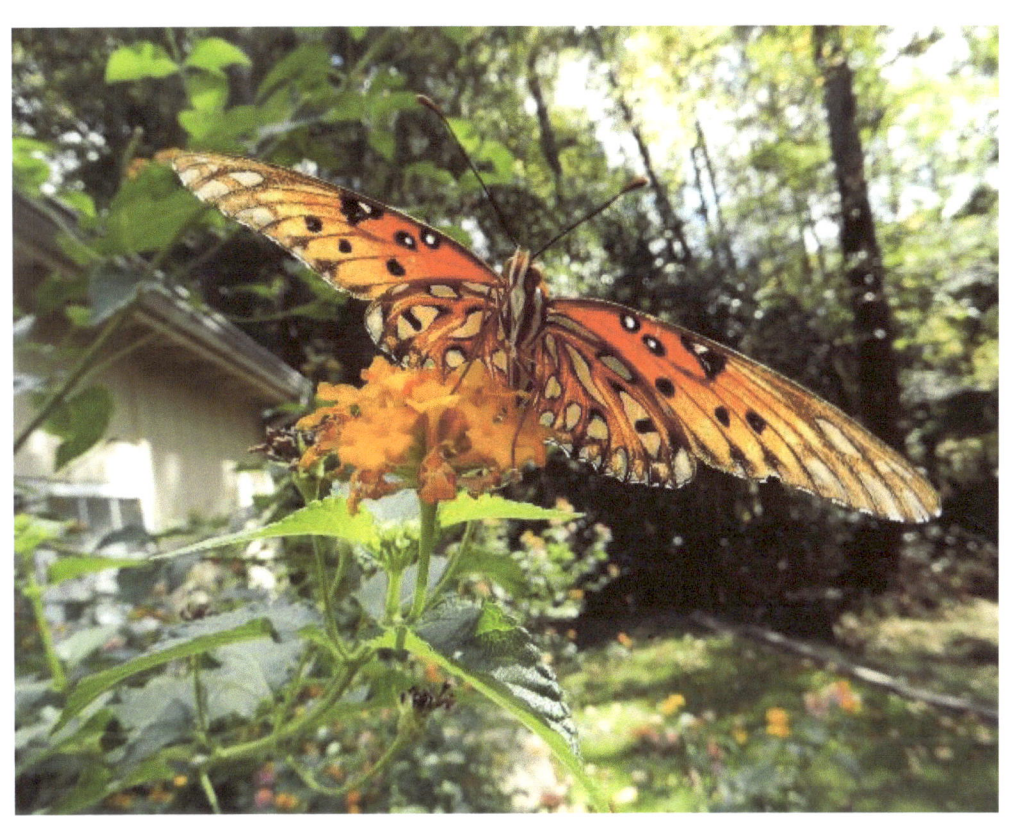

Harriet B. Harris

Published by: Circle of Support, Inc.—A Private, Non-profit Corporation, Established in 1998. Mission: Assisting & Inspiring People to Move Forward

Thecircleofsupport.org

Harrisharriet00@gmail.com

All Rights Reserved. No part of this publication may be reproduced, distributed, or transmitted in any form or by any means, including photocopying, recording or other electronic or mechanical methods, without the prior written permission of the publisher. For permission requests, write to the publisher, addressed above: Attention: Permissions Coordinator.

The photos in this book are for the enjoyment of the reader and should not be copied or in any way used, reproduced, or distributed by the reader.

ISBN: 978-1-7353169-2-5

Library of Congress Control Number: 2024906663

Copyright © 2024, Harriet B. Harris, Author, Photographer, Layout Designer

Cover Photo Title: "Life is Calling" The Gulf Fritillary Butterfly, Author's Backyard

Dedication

To My Grandmother, Georgia Malcolm Bess

She taught me how to plant

beautiful flowers to welcome Butterflies

all Summer Long!

Introduction: Why I Love Butterflies

I have loved Butterflies since I was a young girl working in the yard planting flowers with my grandmother. She loved gardening! Most every Saturday was spent working outdoors making hers the most beautiful gardens in the neighborhood. There was no Home Depot or Lowes back then. Every flower had to be grown from seeds or bulbs, most often saved from the year before. The Zinnia were one of her favorites. This flower is a magnet for butterflies. There was never a time when we did not have lots of these magnificent creatures in our yard. I became very skilled at walking up and capturing them between my fingers. Whenever my young cousins visited us, their immediate request was for me to catch butterflies for them. I never disappointed, capturing the exotic, iridescent winged beauties beneath my fingers.

One day, as I was attempting to fill a glass jar with them (having punched holes in the lid to make what I thought would be a nice new home for them); my grandmother stopped me with this question: "Would you want to live in a jar or live free?" Of course, my immediate response was: "I want to live free". Her raised eyebrow and coy smile looking at my jar, told me the butterflies wanted freedom too. From that day forward, I never captured a butterfly with my hands again. But my fascination with these lovely, delicate creatures has stayed with me all my life!

Several years ago, upon learning photography I found a way to 'capture' their beauty again! Using the same technique I learned as a child, walking quietly upon them, blending into their environment, not making big, threatening moves; they became mine again in beautiful photos! You see, like most creatures, butterflies are very adept at realizing when they are in danger. They know how to avoid spider webs, know how to fly away from birds (who they know will eat them), and can quickly avoid anyone trying to swat them.

However, when they realize our presence is not at all threatening, they will relax and allow a closer look. Thus, without telephoto lenses, or touching them, I can take photos of them as they go about their life!

Like my grandmother, I learned to plant Zinnia and other flowers which they enjoy. This allows me to attract large numbers of butterflies to my sunny, quiet backyard! Their calming presence reminds me of the days I spent gardening with my grandmother, learning the patience and skills needed to nurture life into existence! To me there are few things more satisfying than seeing a seedling burst through the soil and become something beautiful, which attracts something even more glorious! The butterflies teach us to enjoy the beauty we see daily, beauty which we too can bring into this world!

Harriet B. Harris, Inspirational Photographer

Table of Contents

1. Bringing Shameless Beauty Wherever We Go 11

2. Soaring Beyond Dreams 21

3. Hope is Freedom 29

4. Songs of Southern Gardens 39

5. More Than Surviving—Thriving 53

6. "Like the Butterflies: Go Wherever You Please
   & Please Wherever You Go"! 63

7. About the Author 75

8. Acknowledgements 76

9. Review 77

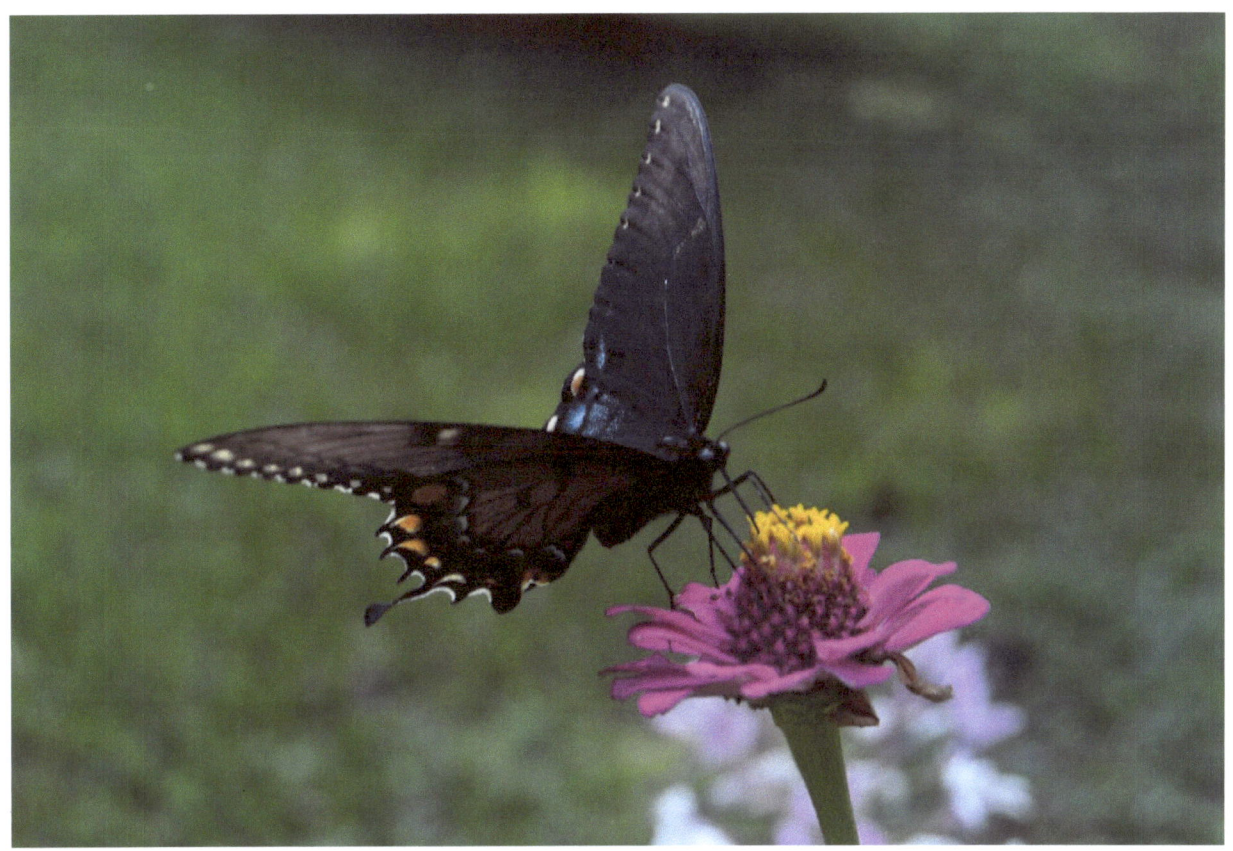

"Fearless Black Beauty" Black Swallowtail

A beautiful shot from my backyard!

Bring Shameless Beauty Wherever We Go!

The Butterfly is nature's most enchanting insect. There are more than 17,000 different varieties the world over. Each continent and many countries have their own unique specimens, shamelessly presenting an endless variety of beauty.

But it is important to realize that from the standpoint of the Butterfly, shamelessly presenting its beauty is all that it knows how to do! It does not consciously spend time preparing to be beautiful. It does not compare itself to or imitate other creatures. It does not regret having not been born something else. It instinctively knows its place in the world, and effortlessly fits into it. It is born with all the potential to be its delightful self; and to live life according to the marvelous design of its Creator!

So, if we will only 'listen' to the Butterflies, we too will bring Shameless Beauty Wherever We Go!

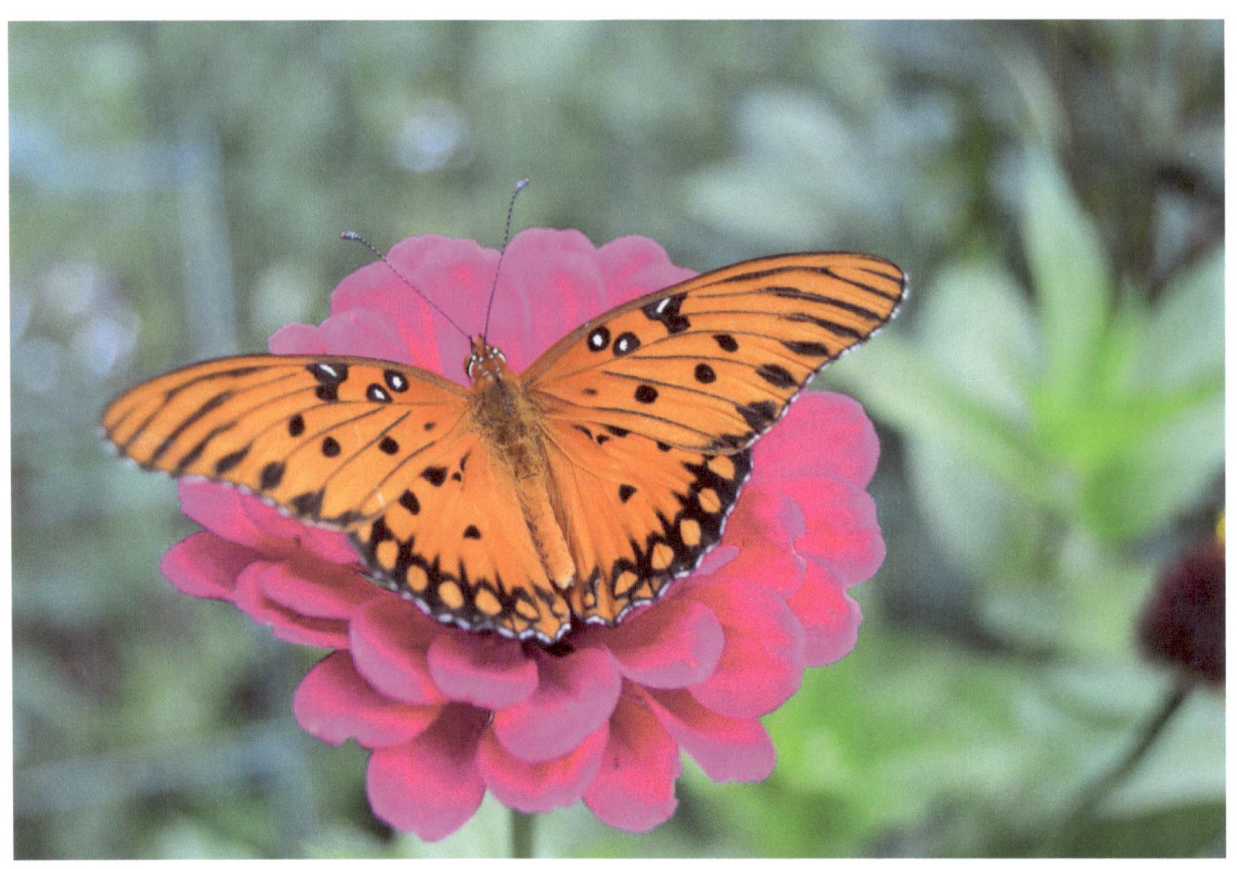

"Pretty on Pink"   Gulf Fritillary on Zinnia Flower

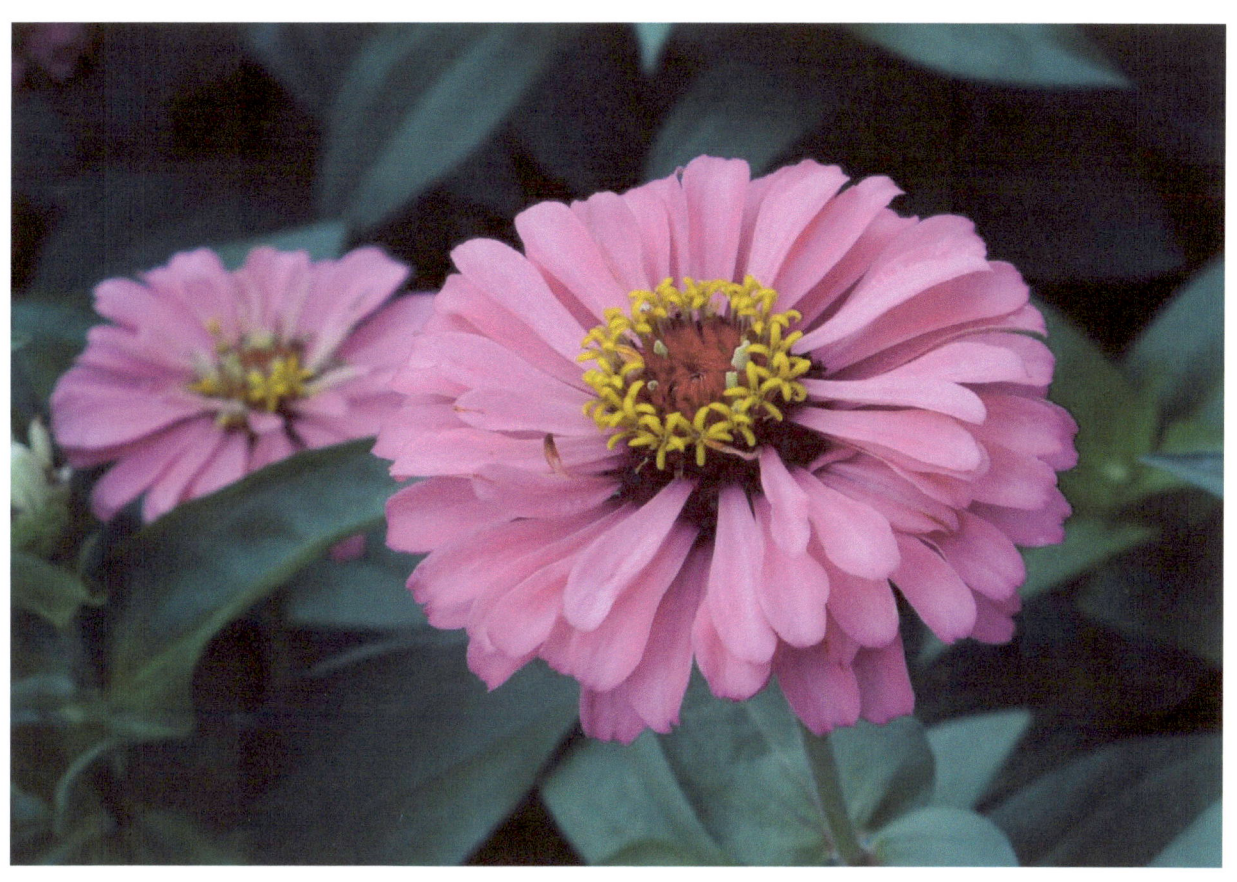

Zinnia flowers grow easily from seeds.
Begin them together in a pot, then thin once
they begin to grow & transplant them into the soil once
they are approximately three inches tall—
once they bloom, wait for the butterflies!

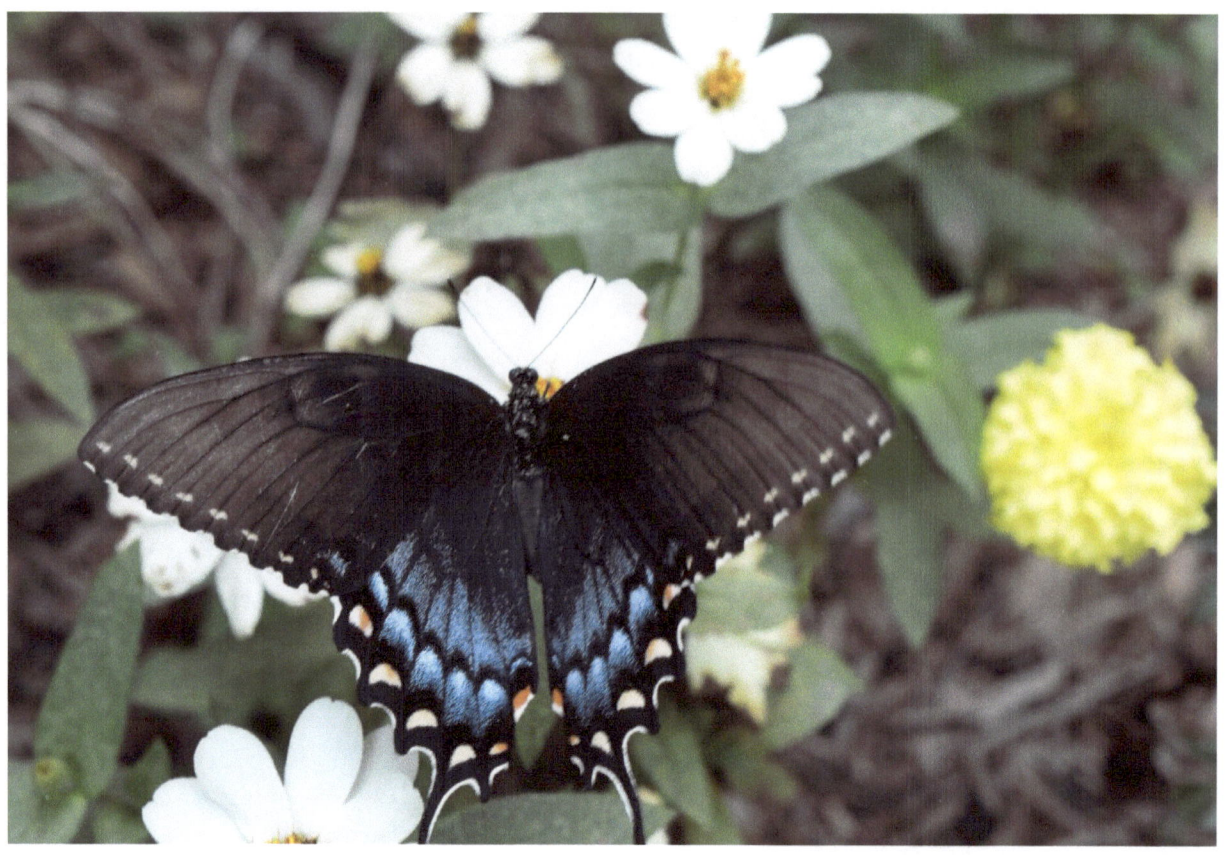

"Enjoying Morning" #3   Black Swallowtail Female

The ladies most often are more colorful & ornate,

ladies bring the bling!

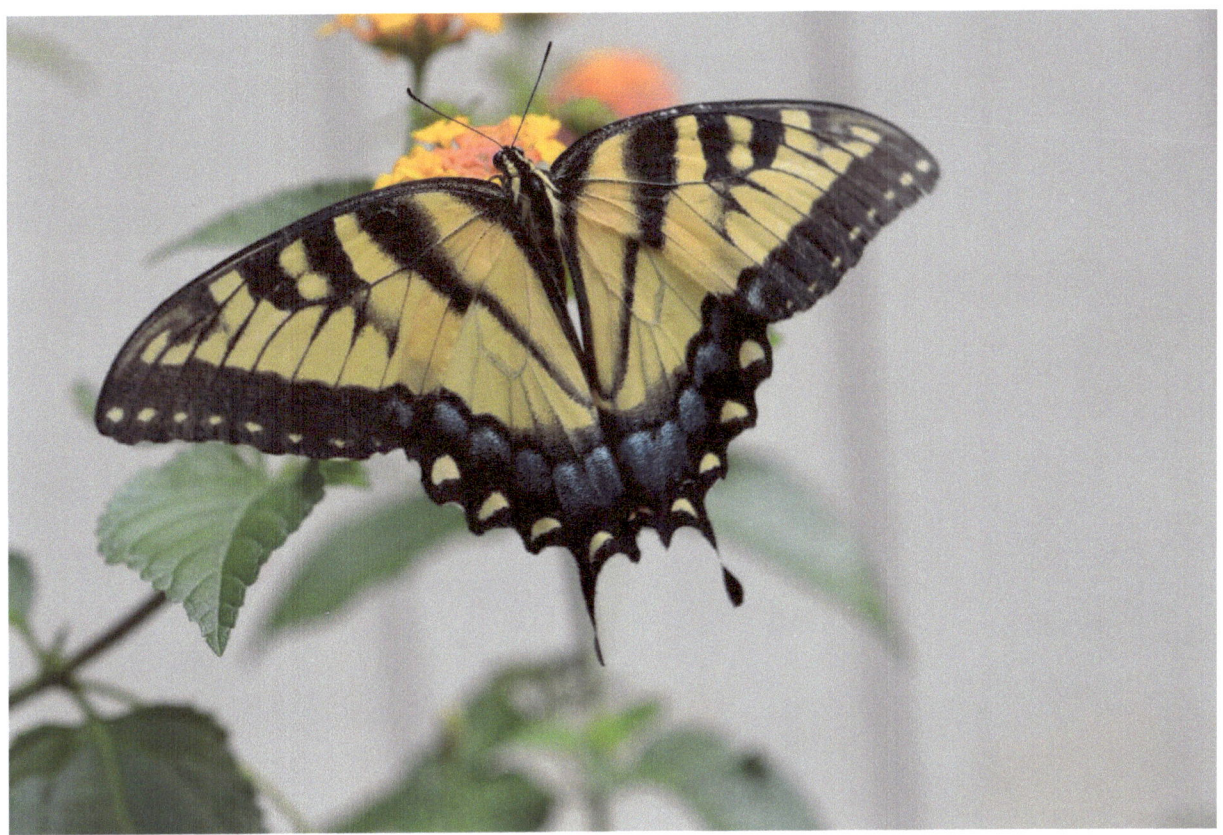

"Morning Glory" Tiger Swallowtail Female

Lantana plants will re-grow each year.
Wait to cut them back in the spring, only
after the danger of frost has passed.

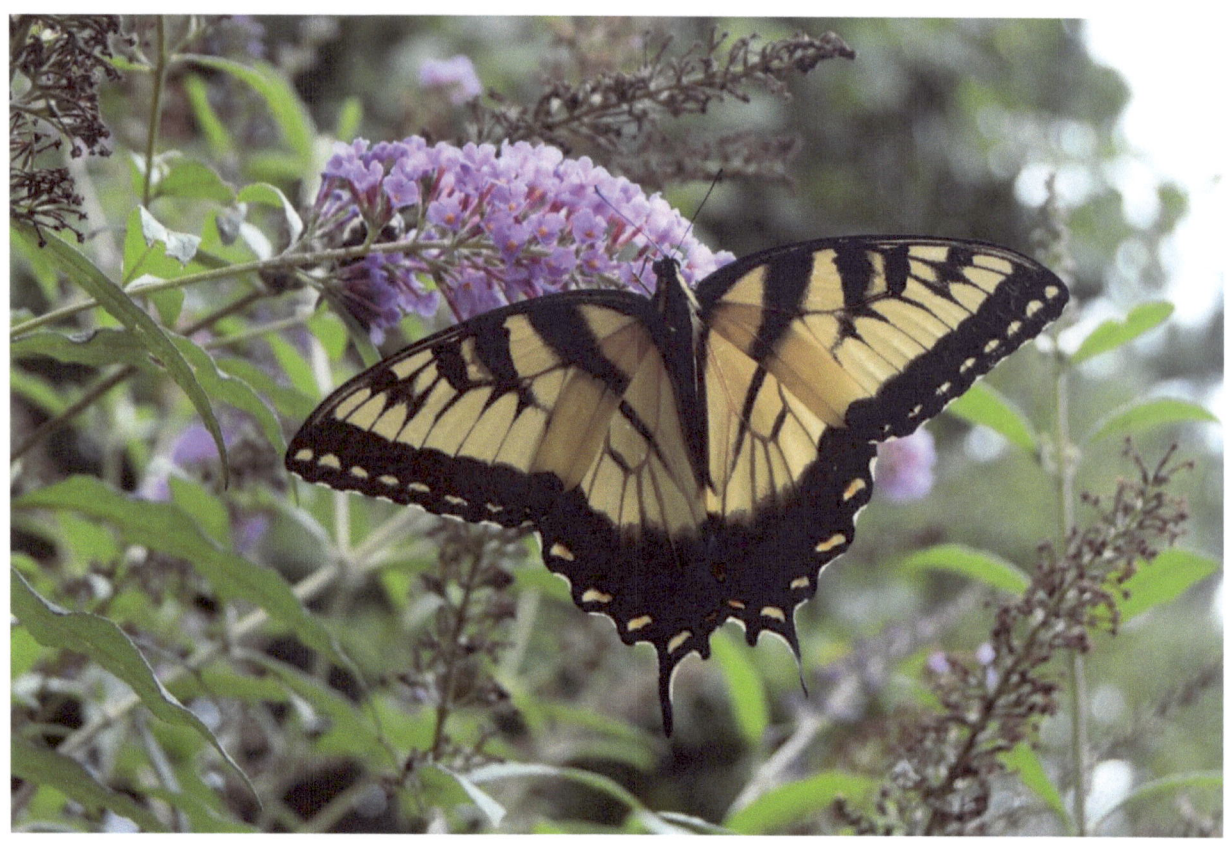

"Good Morning!" Tiger Swallowtail Male

Shot taken on a Butterfly Bush

in front of my front door!

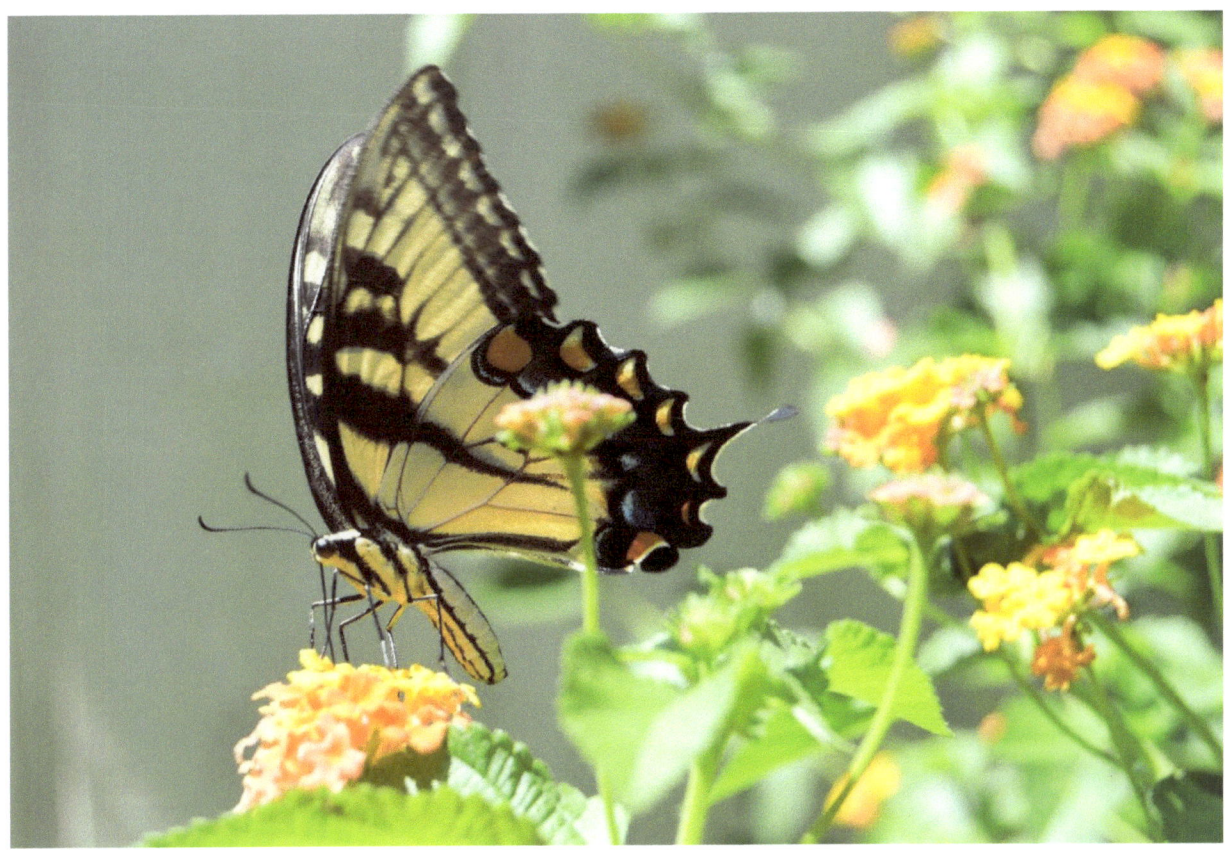

"Morning Glory #2" Tiger Swallowtail Female

I observe these beauties frequently

returning for 2nds & 3rds throughout the day!

They especially enjoy the nectar & morning dew

on these plants!

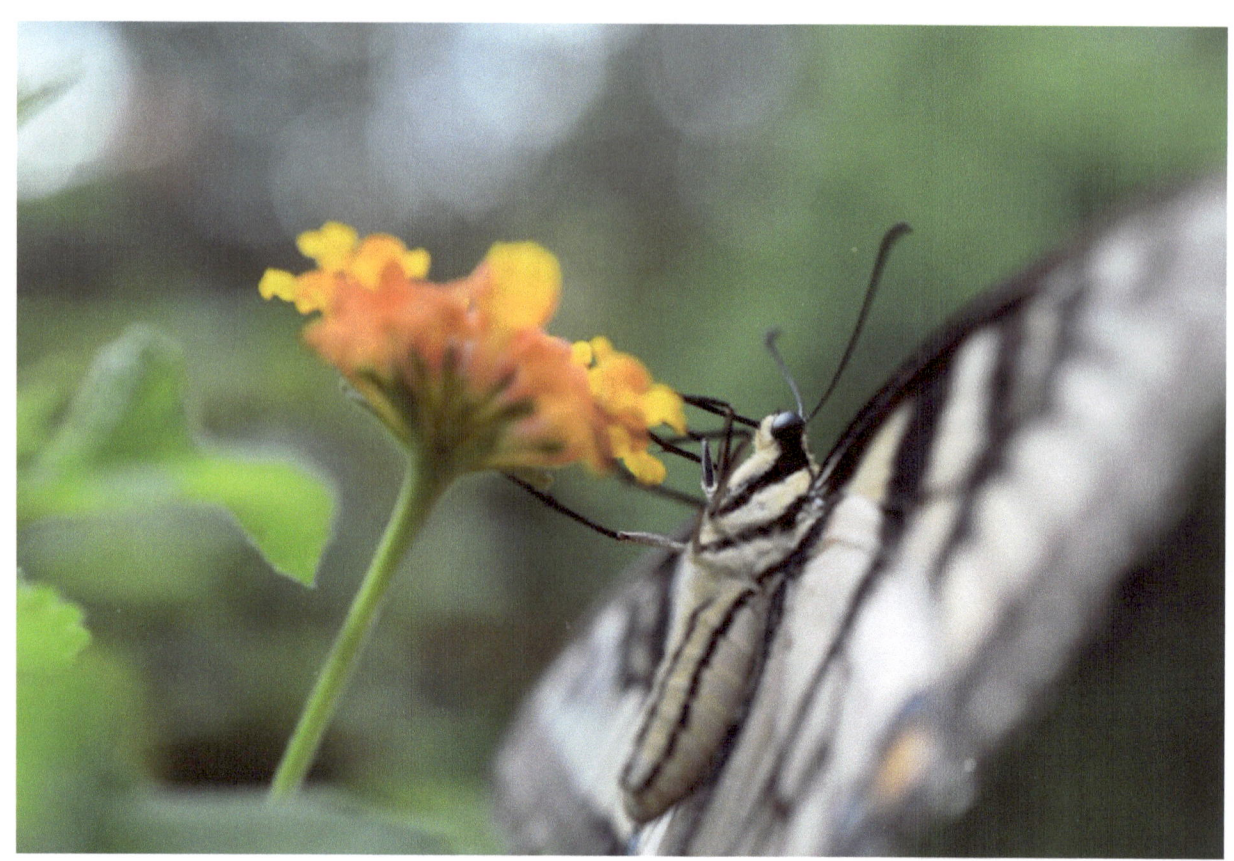

Notice how it pays me no attention

as I stand just a foot or two away!

The Tiger Swallowtail butterfly is the State Butterfly
of Georgia. It can be seen most frequently around
areas containing poplar trees, prickly ash, and
citrus trees, where it lays its eggs.
My backyard contains many poplar trees.

It is interesting to note that each butterfly lays
its eggs on particular trees or plants. For instance, the
Monarch butterfly lays its eggs on the leaves of the
milkweed plant, their only caterpillar host plant.

Each species of butterflies follows its Creator's unique design
to ensure their propagation & thus their survival.

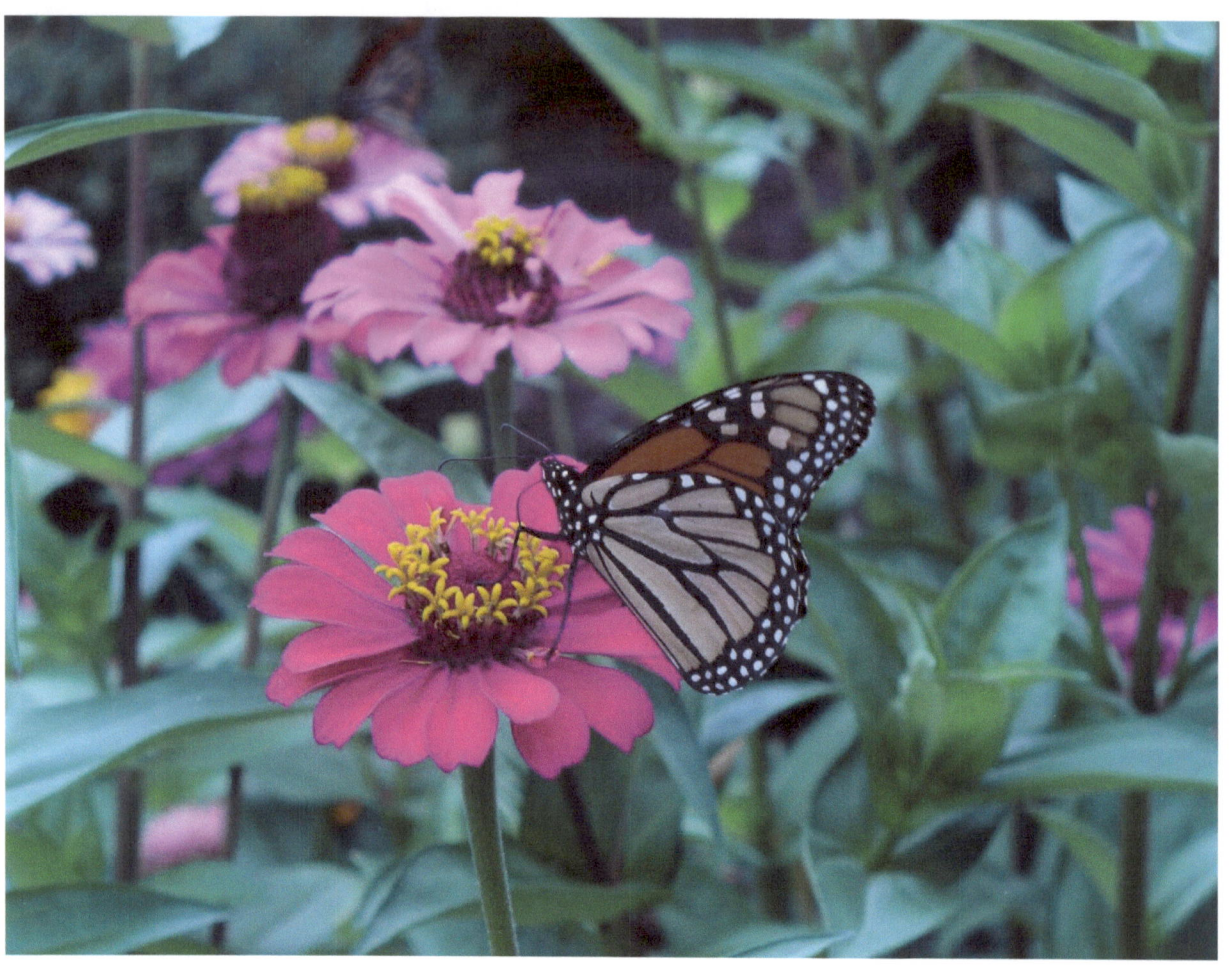

"Summer Garden"   The Monarch

I ran into this beauty at a highway rest stop in Tennessee.

It stopped for a Zinnia snack,

while taking a break from the long trek from Canada to Mexico.

Soaring Beyond Dreams

What I have learned about the Monarch butterfly is incredible! These creatures make a year-long journey from Canada to Mexico. In my research, I learned that millions of these winged creatures navigate their way for some 3,000 miles each from Canada to Mexico in the fall, and vice-versa in the spring, without losing their way! I was utterly amazed by their innate ability to follow this pattern year after year.

Upon further research, I learned that the Monarchs that begin in Canada are actually the grand and great-grand parents of the butterflies that arrive in Mexico! You see, the Monarch only has a lifespan of 6-8 weeks. However, their journey can take two to three months to complete. So, many of the Monarchs that begin the journey are not the ones who complete it; as they are laying eggs and generating new ones along the way! Imagine the incredible determination of this species to complete a journey which their ancestors began—a journey which was only a dream of their fore-parents.

This is such an impressive example for us. How much do we think about or work toward completing a journey or a dream of those who came before us? It is often quoted from Maya Angelou's poem: "*Still I Rise*": "Bringing the gifts that my ancestors gave, I am the dream and the hope of the slave". May we too "rise" in our determination to always press forward!

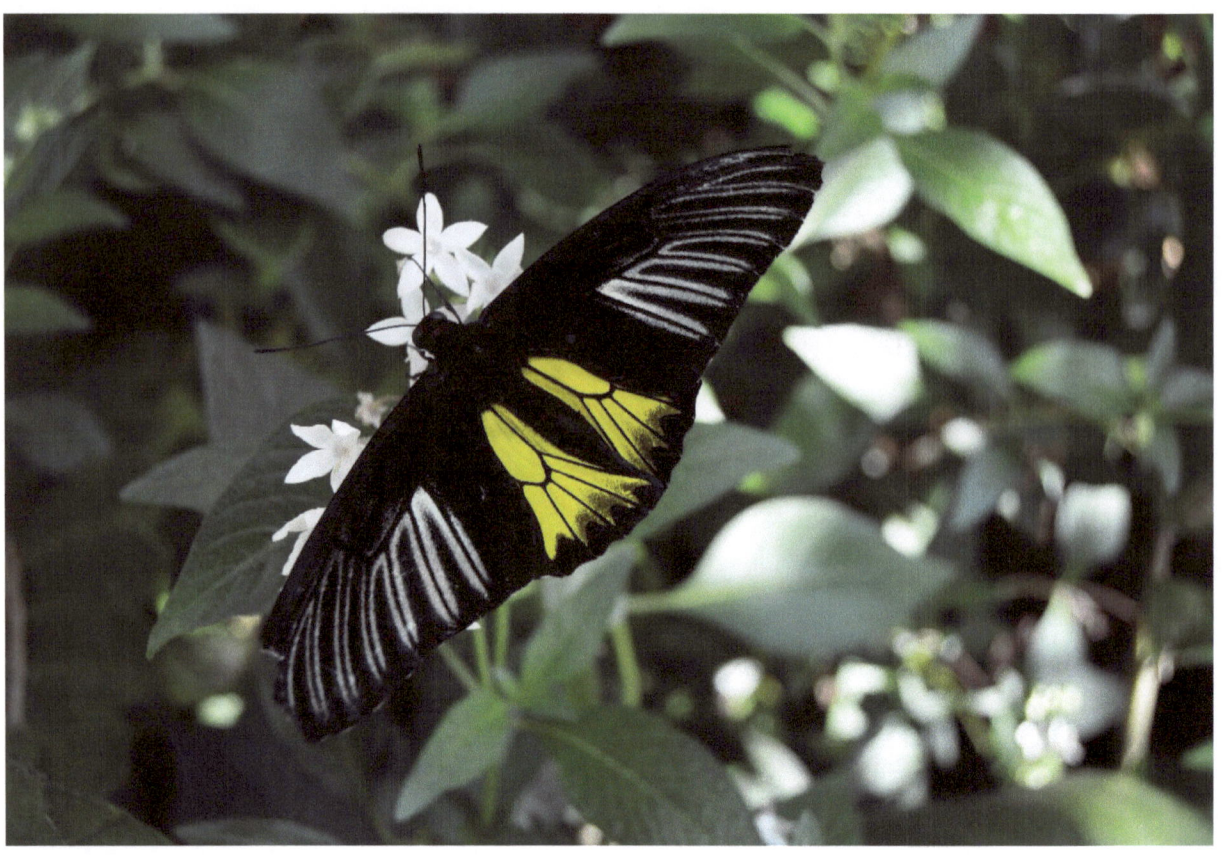

"Ready for Flight"   Golden Birdwing

The Longwings and Birdwing Butterflies

can have a wingspan of up to nine inches across.

These beauties are built for speed!

(I found several varieties at Georgia's Callaway Gardens)

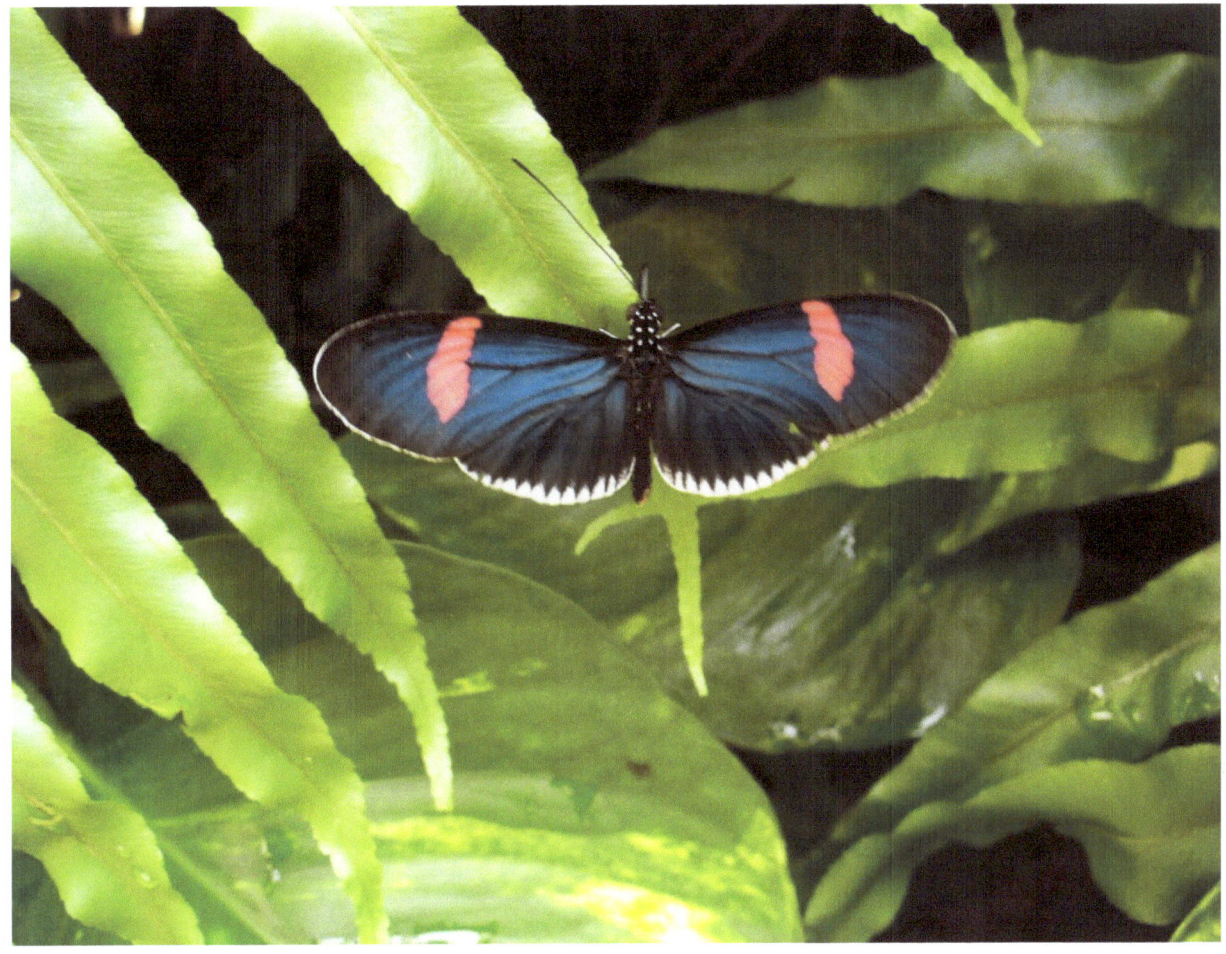

"We Wear the Mask"　　　　　　　　　　　　　　　　Erato Longwing

If you look closely at the head of this image

you will see why I gave it this name.

(It looks like an African mask with head-dress)

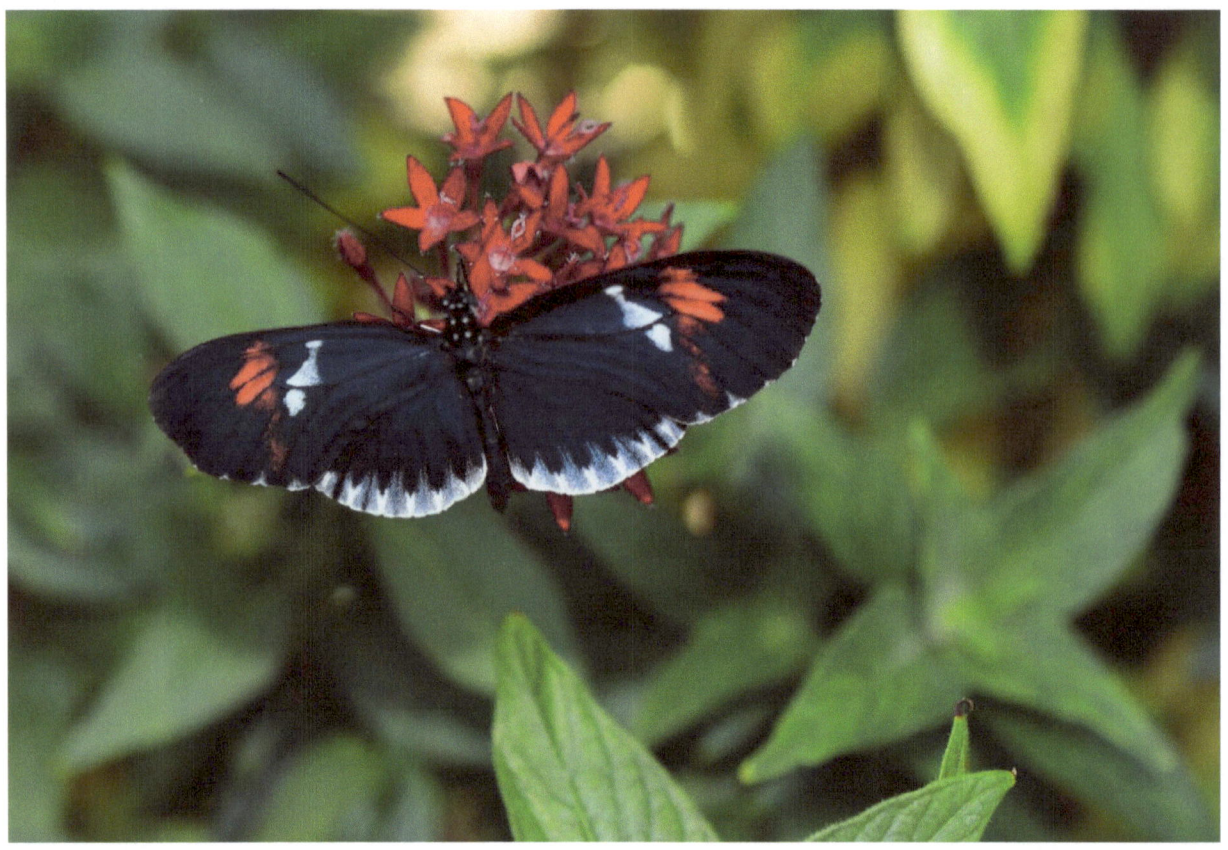

"And Still, I Rise"   Crimson Patch Longwing

There are about fifty distinct species of

Heliconia or Longwing Butterflies on the planet

Their distinctive markings vary from place to place.

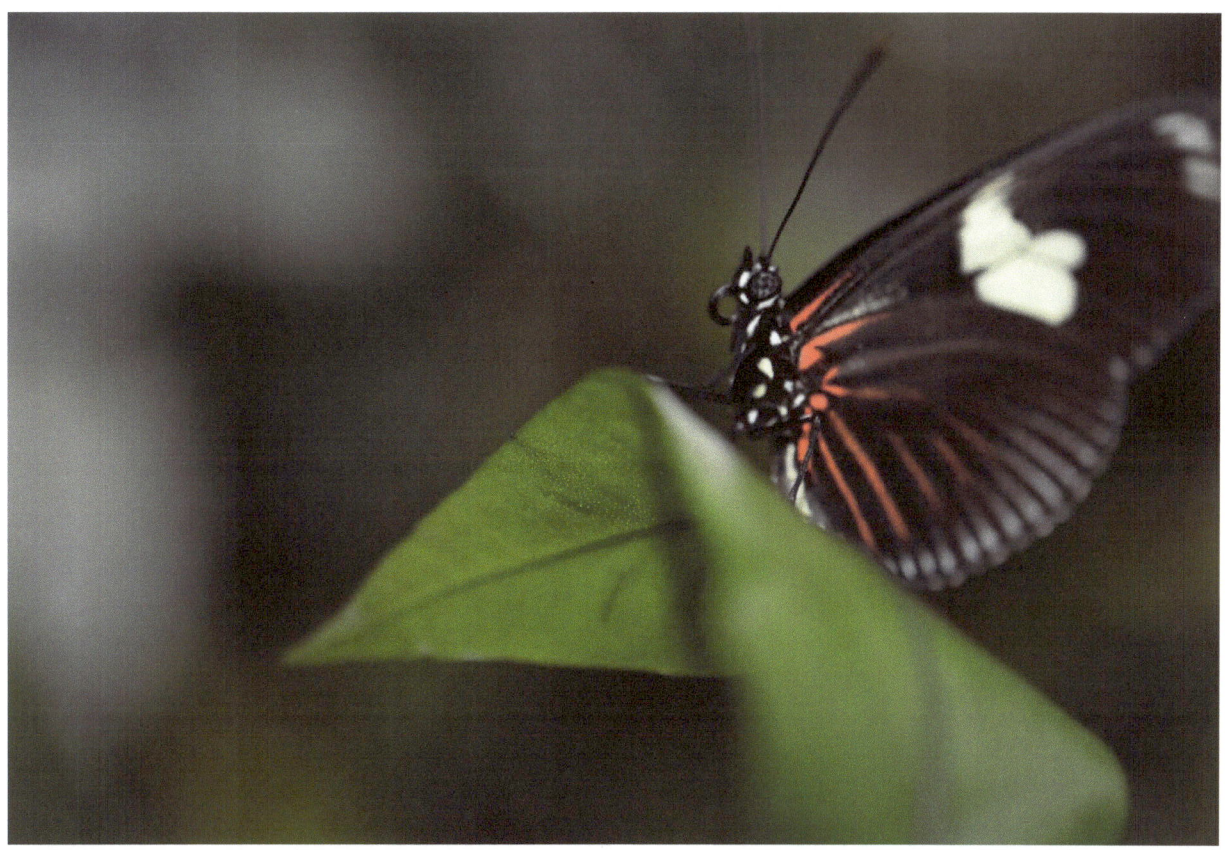

"Watching me, Watching you" Crimson Patch Longwing

Notice the compound eye—dozens of
mini eyes, which enables them to see movement
all around their bodies; this helps them ward off danger.

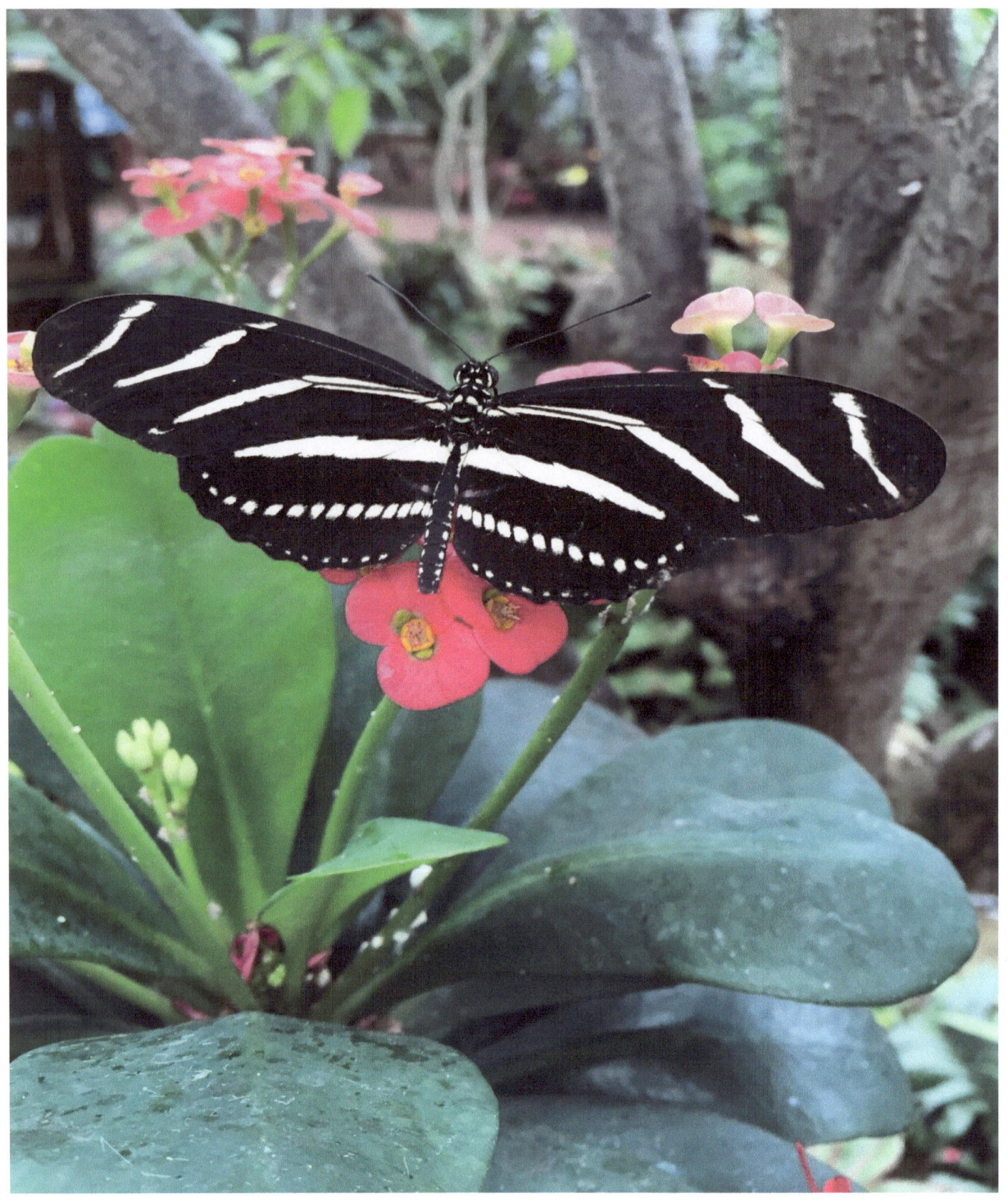

"Zebra Beauty"   Zebra Striped Longwing

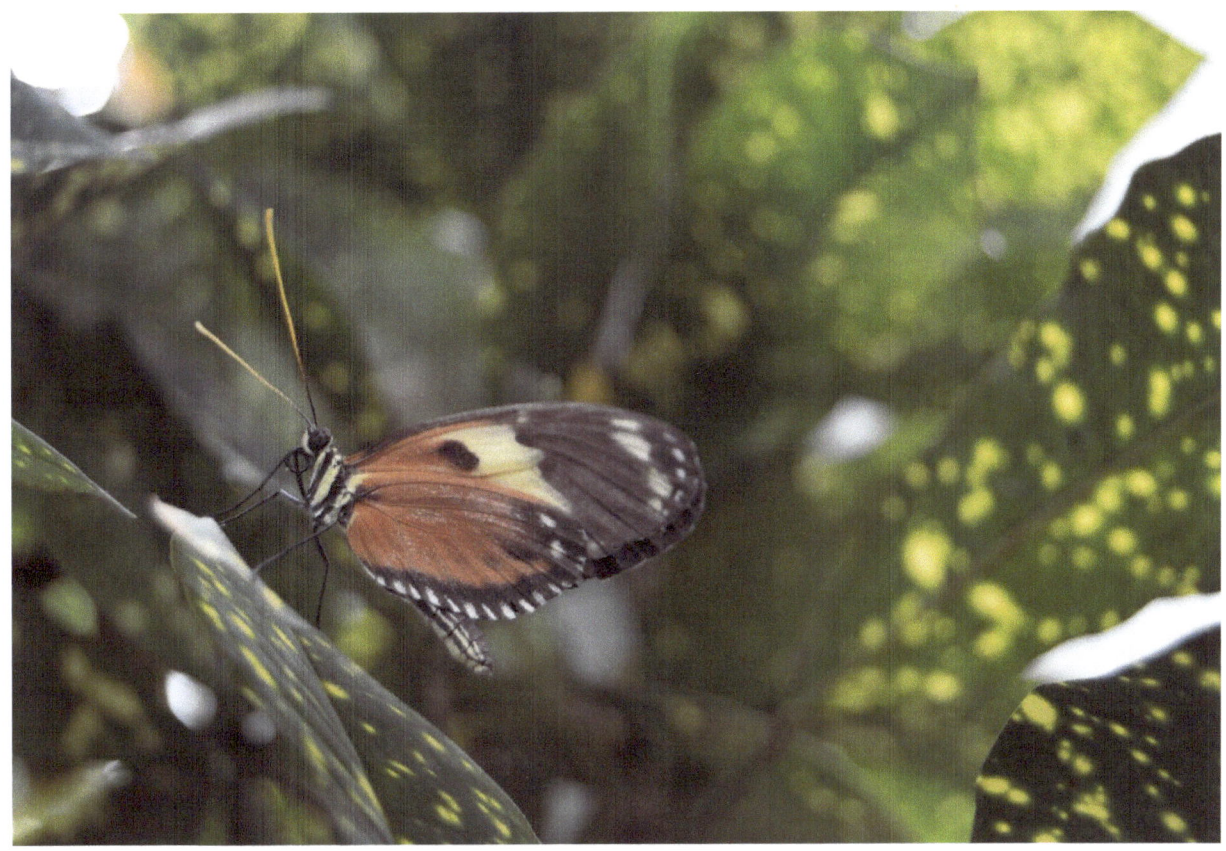

"Eyes All Around Us" Tiger Longwing

Listen to the Butterflies—Hope is Freedom!

In the world today, there are many people losing hope for a brighter future. Many times, we hear people lamenting how difficult life is becoming. So much of what we focus on is negative. Much of what we see in the media causes us to compare ourselves to others and see lack instead of adequacy or abundance. Real and perceived slights confront us daily, causing a sense of despair and hopelessness. Many people, if asked if they could turn things around, focus on what others are doing or not doing to their liking. So much of our happiness is tied to what others do, or do not do on our behalf.

But if we could only stop and really look around us, we would see things which let us know that "hope springs eternal", as the saying goes. Daily the physical environment, reflecting change and growth, testifies to the fact that a new start is always possible!

The butterfly is a notable example: Here is a creature which goes through four (4) stages of life, looking completely different in every stage, before it is mature. It starts from a tiny egg, the size of a pin head, laid on the leaves of a plant. It then becomes a caterpillar. The caterpillar first feeds on the shell from which it is born, and then the surrounding leaves. The caterpillar sheds its skin several times as it grows bigger. Once it is big enough, it stops eating and covers itself with a protective layer, the chrysalis. It is then known as the pupa, a tube-like wad made of mostly liquid. The pupa instinctively adopts the color of the surrounding foliage, so that it is protected from harm, as it hangs motionless on the underside of a leaf. Inside the chrysalis, it undergoes changes for about ten days; and finally emerges, having become the beautiful creature which we see flying around. From a tiny spec on the bottom of a leaf, the butterfly morphs into a creature which inherently knows its perfect place in nature; having within itself exactly what is needed to live a beautiful life! It then flies freely, knowing its place of splendor in the world.

I believe that we are a lot more like butterflies than we know. We go through several stages of life also: infants, childhood, young adulthood, mature adulthood. But our metamorphosis does not always create beauty. Perhaps we get outside our natural elements (so to speak), by allowing others to interfere with our positive growth, development, and existence; losing the hope that is instinctively ours.

Remember, the butterfly follows its instinctive pattern without outside interference. It can therefore become the majestic creature at which we marvel and smile brightly, any time we are lucky enough to come across one!

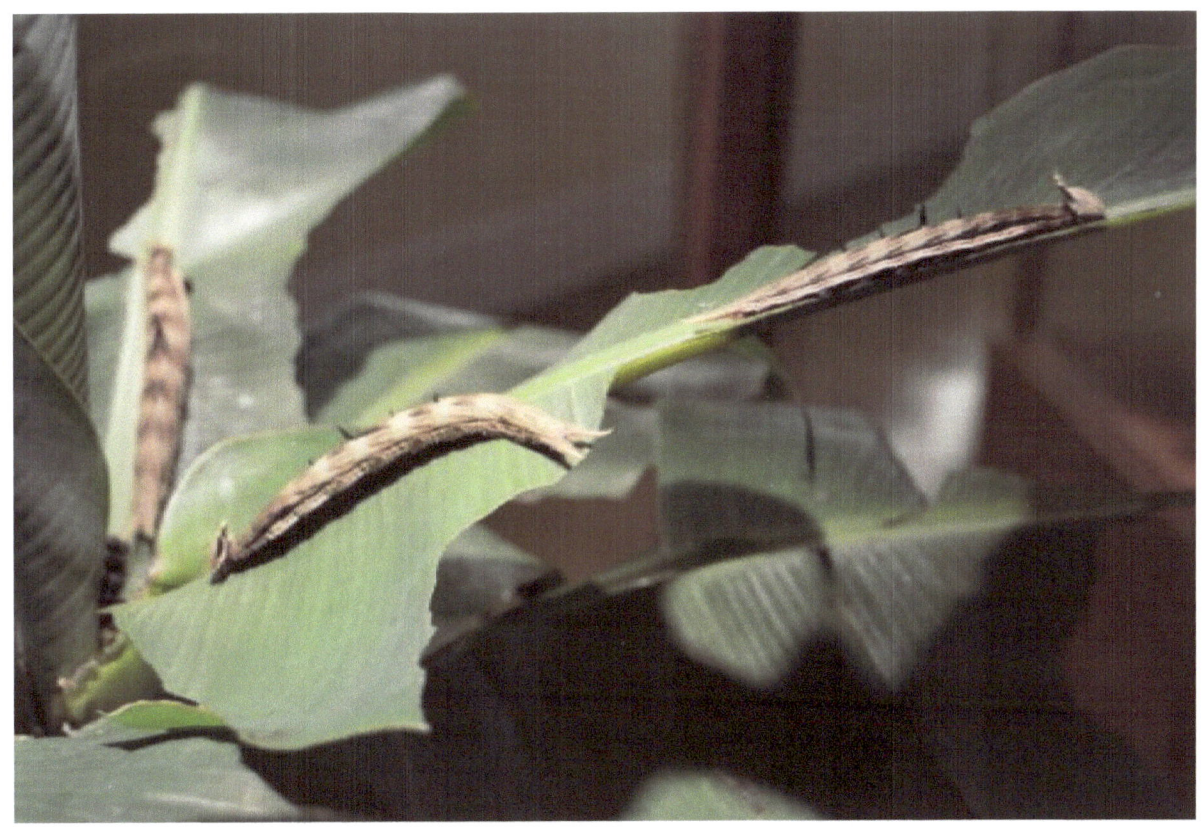

"Lying in Wait"   Owl Butterfly Caterpillars

Callaway Gardens incubates and provides sanctuary

for many varied species.

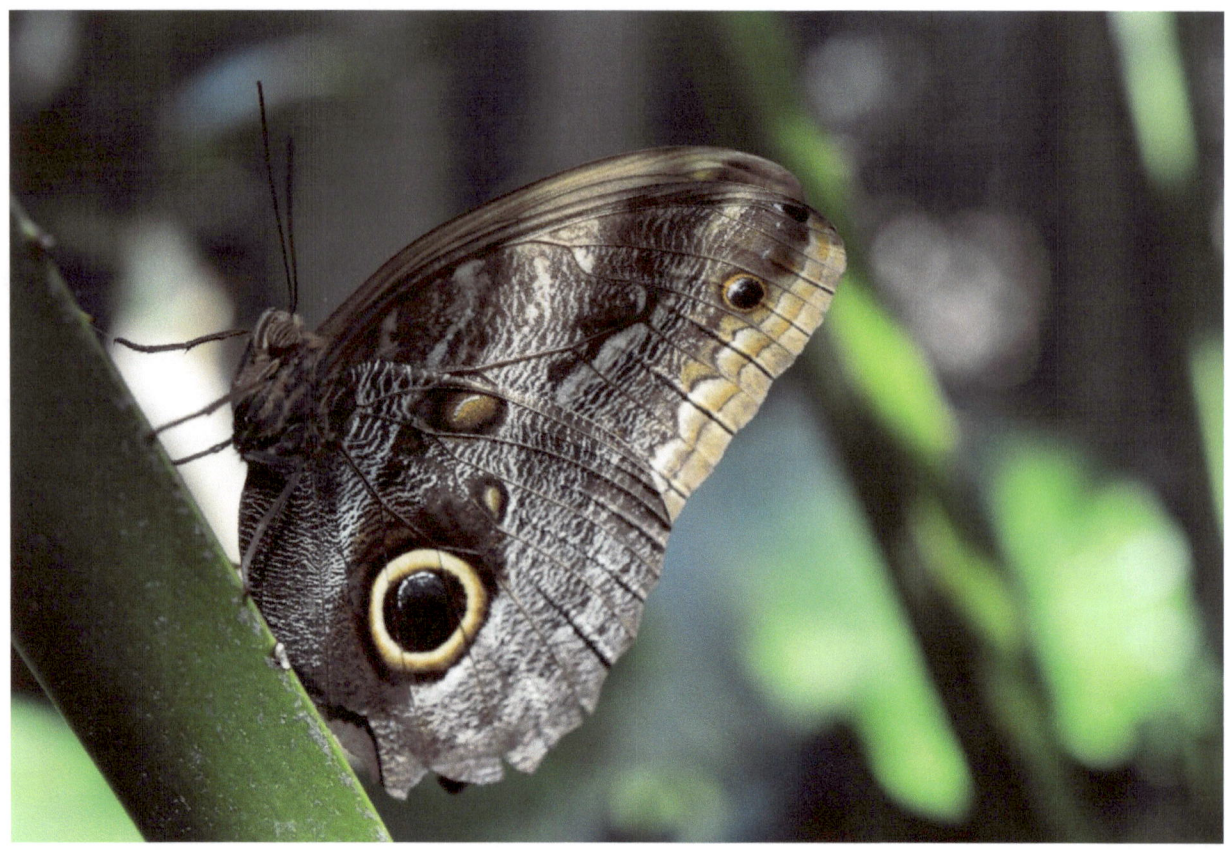

"Night Beauty" Owl Butterfly

Notice it looks like the surrounding landscape. These beauties are masters of camouflage

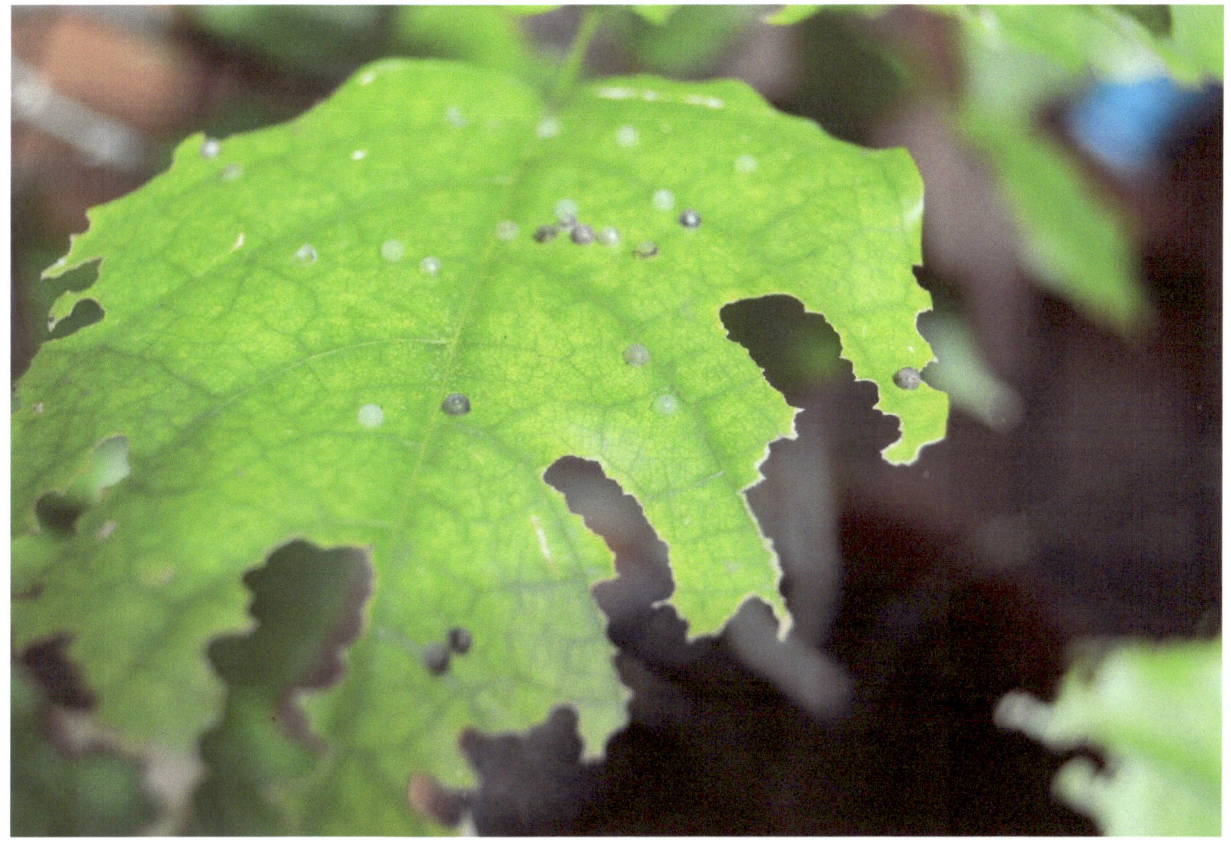

"Potential"   Blue Morpho Eggs

At the Gardens Butterfly Conservatory, the Blue Morpho Butterfly makes a legendary appearance every Fall!

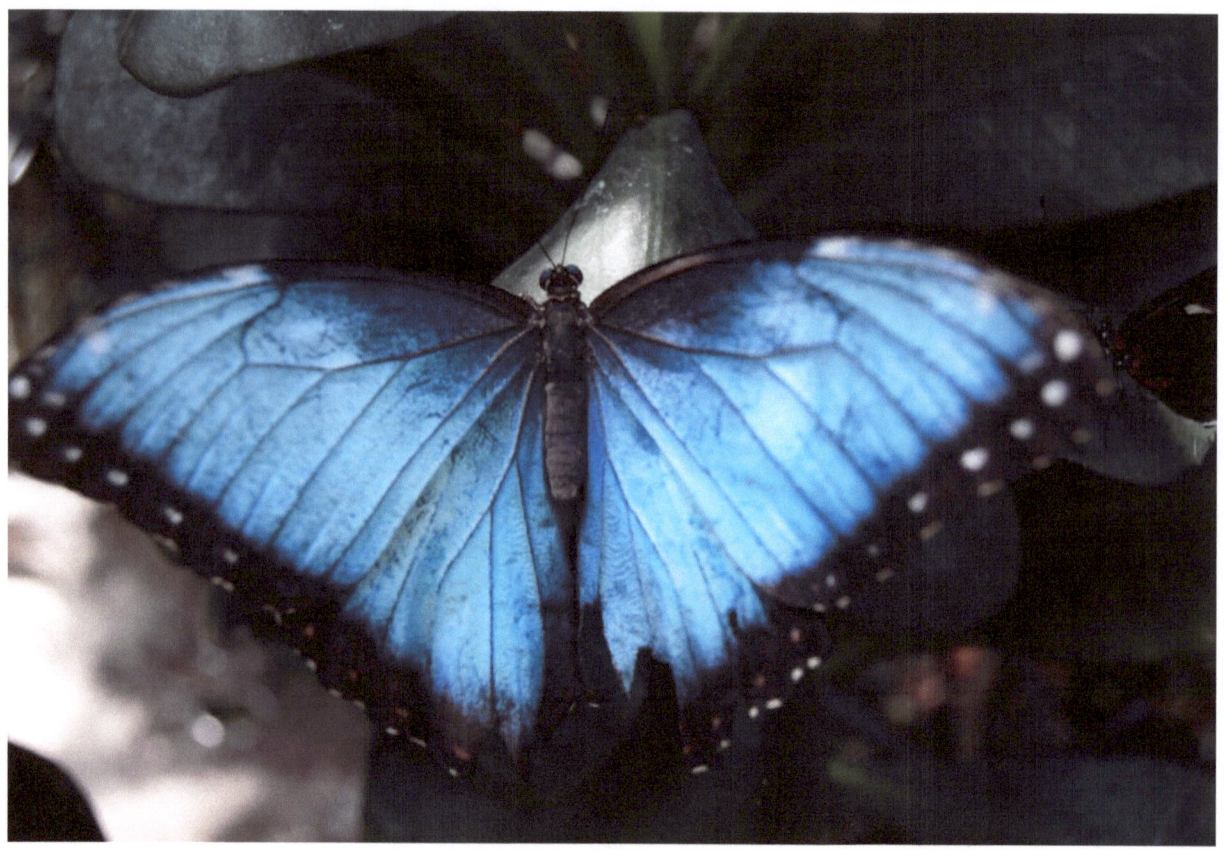

"Blue Majesty #3"   Blue Morpho

There is a mystery surrounding how its bright, shiny color is created. There is no other creature whose color matches it. Note too that the blue color is only on the inside of the wings.

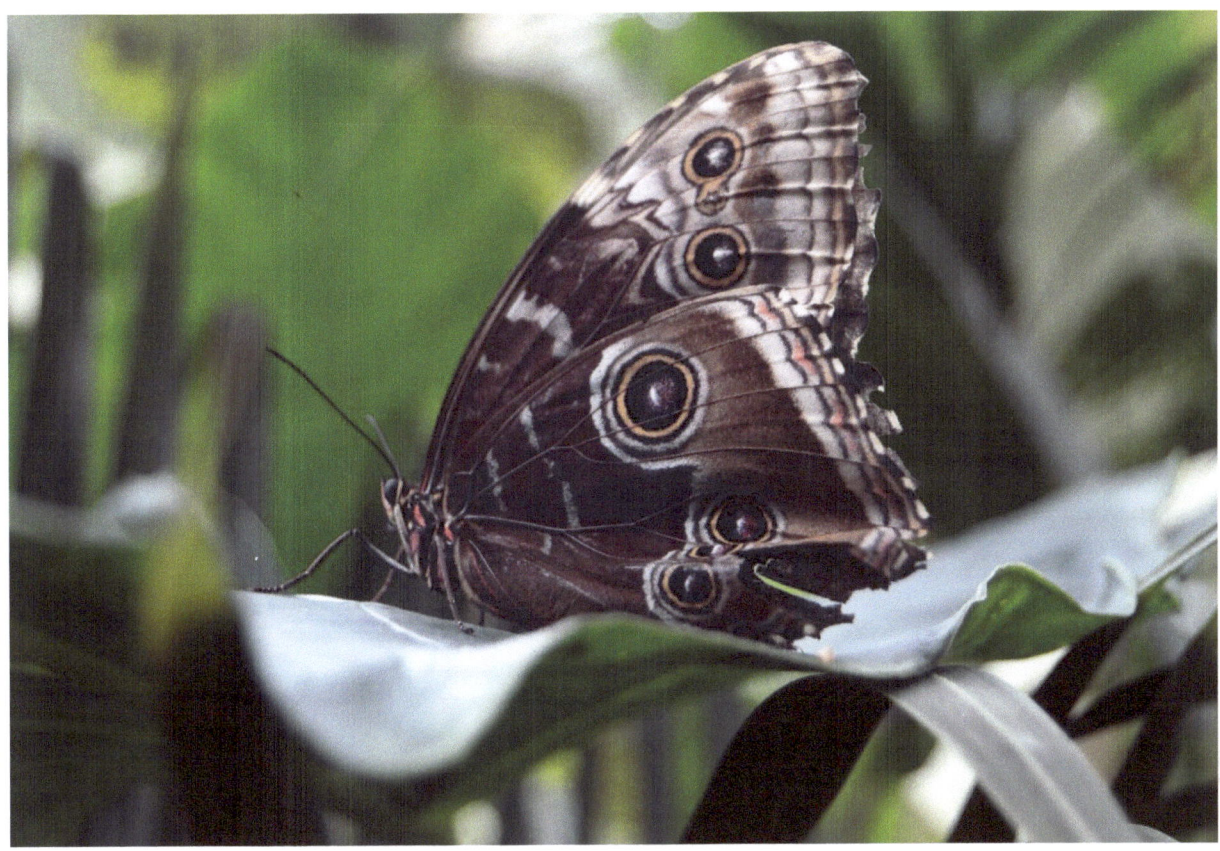

"*Enjoying Morning*" Blue Morpho

The outside of the wings makes this creature

look totally different!

Like the Owl Butterfly, it camouflages well.

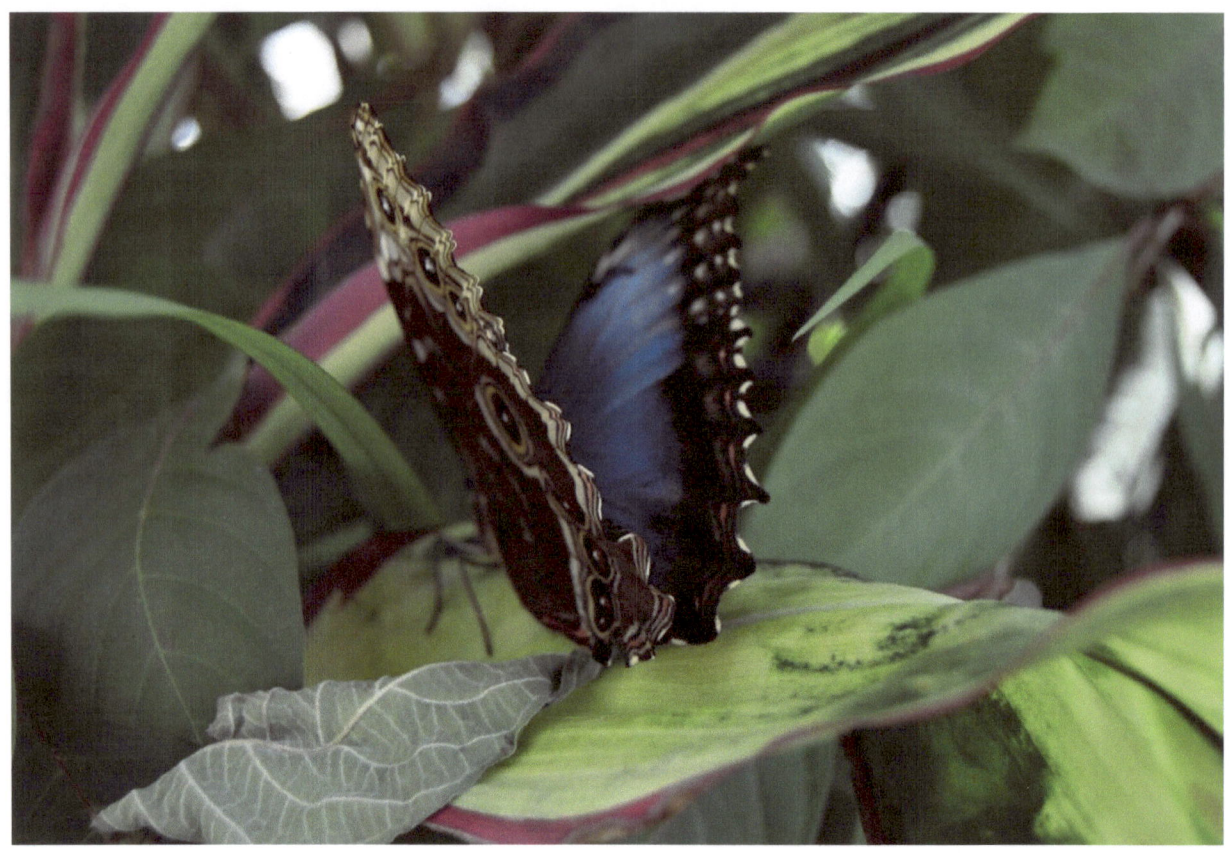

"Hiding Out"   Blue Morpho

This was a rare occasion, capturing both sides of the wings!

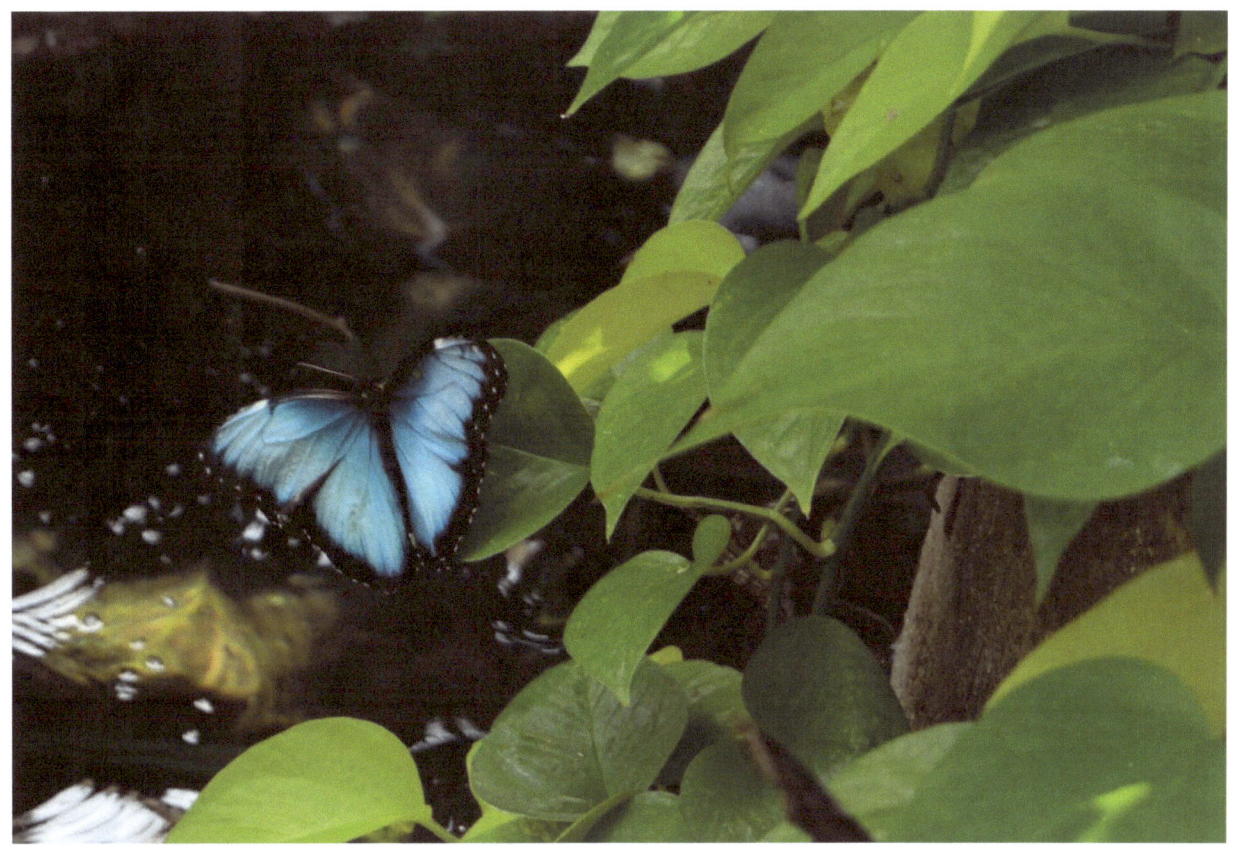

"At the Creek" Blue Morpho

Songs of Southern Gardens

Since I began photographing butterflies, I have always tried to visit places which offers me the opportunity to do so where ever I travel. The butterfly conservatory at Callaway Gardens here in Georgia is one of my favorite places. It houses a large variety of butterflies native to the south. The Swallowtails (Georgia's State butterfly), is in abundance there most every time I visit. But as noted above, the Blue Morpho is also one of their big attractions. In years passed, each fall when these magnificent creatures made their appearance, a wine and cheese reception was held for them. You see, the Blue Morpho actually likes to drink red wine! They will lite on the rim of wine glasses and take sips along with you! The receptions were held in the evening. So these creatures had an opportunity for a "night cap" as they slow and settled down for the evening. The scene was very enchanting!

Another favorite place of mine is Butterfly World in Coconut Creek Florida. This three acre exhibit is the largest in the country. They house a variety of these magnificent creatures both inside and outside, along with an incredible array of flowers and trees. It is a great place to have events such as weddings, receptions, and parties year-round.

These are just two of many Southern Gardens available to all who care to visit these awesome creatures. The following are some shots from Butterfly World:

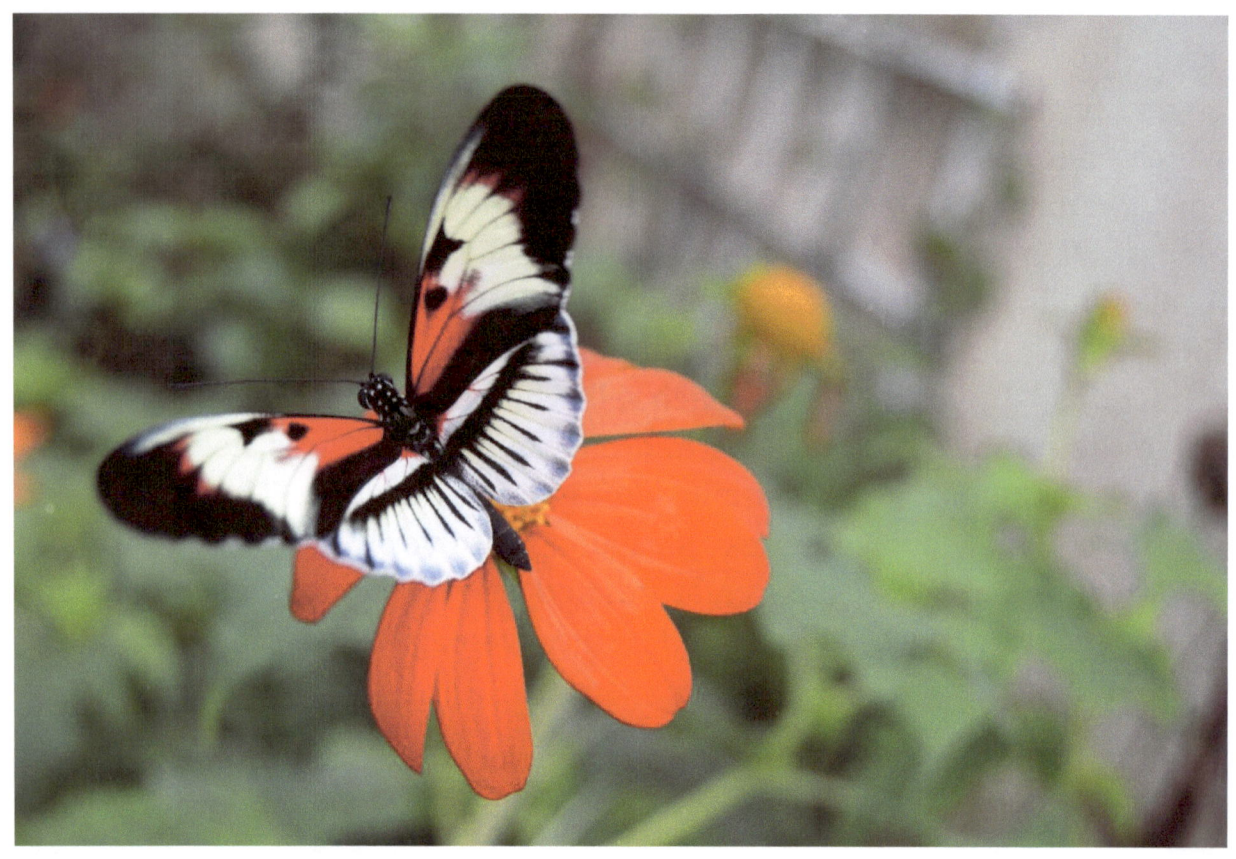

"Beauty on Orange" — Postman Butterfly

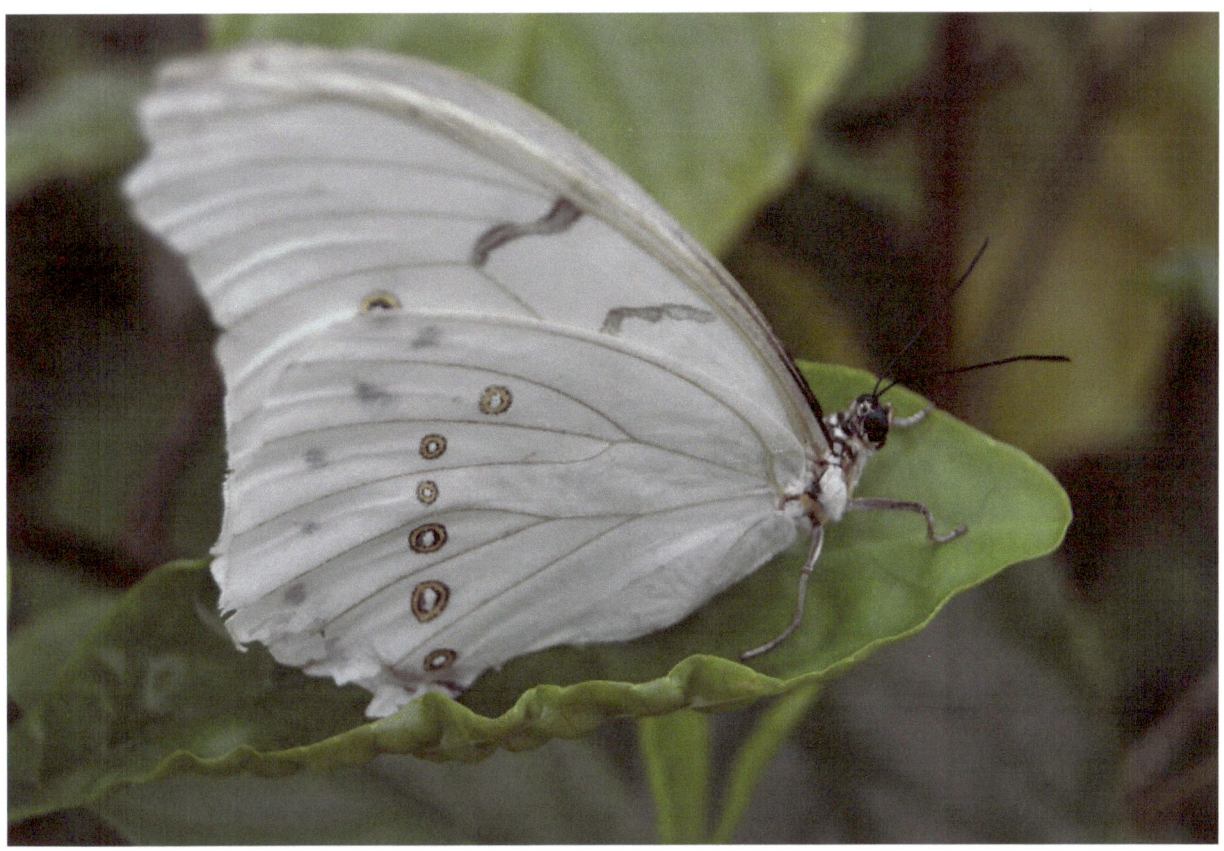

"Beauty in Beige"   White Morpho

This beauty is a cousin to the Blue Morpho,

both species have blue eyes!

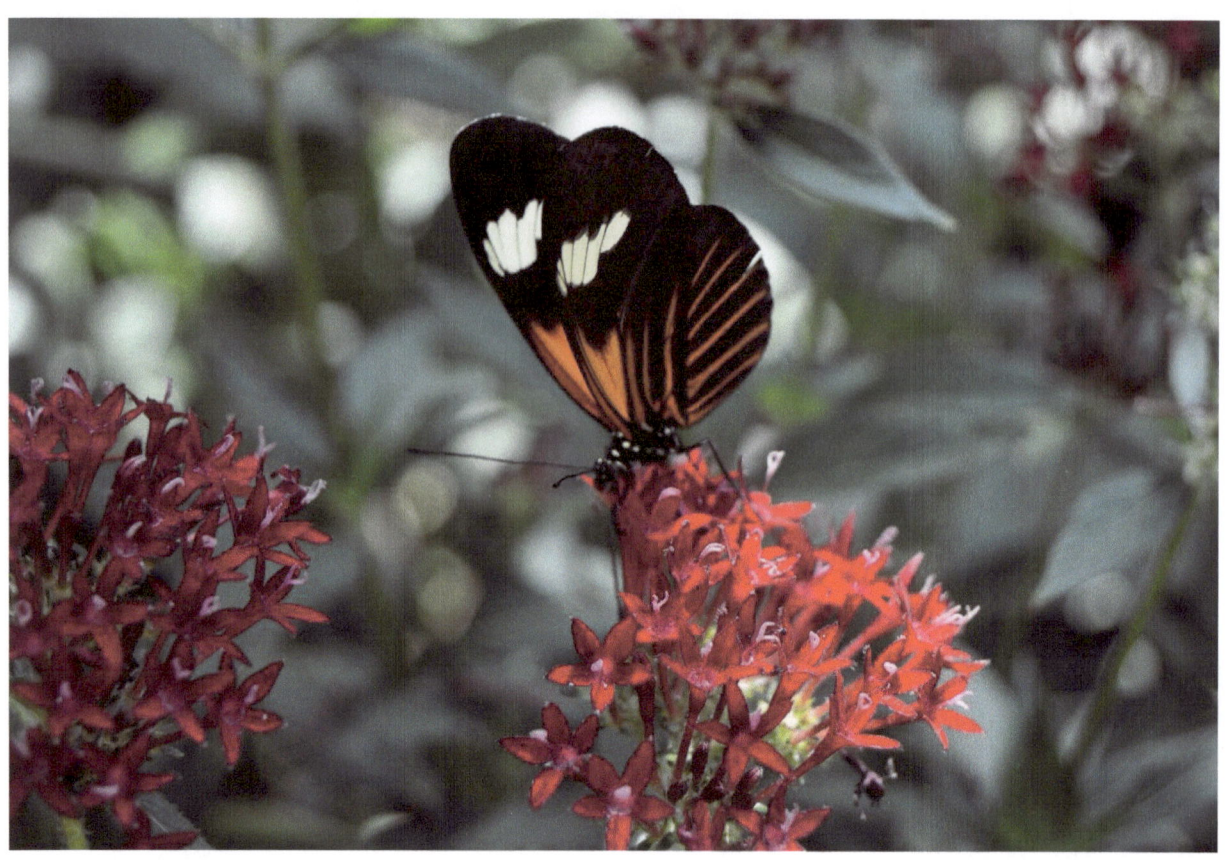

"*I Love Morning*" #2   Postman Butterfly

This beauty is a part of the

Longwing family

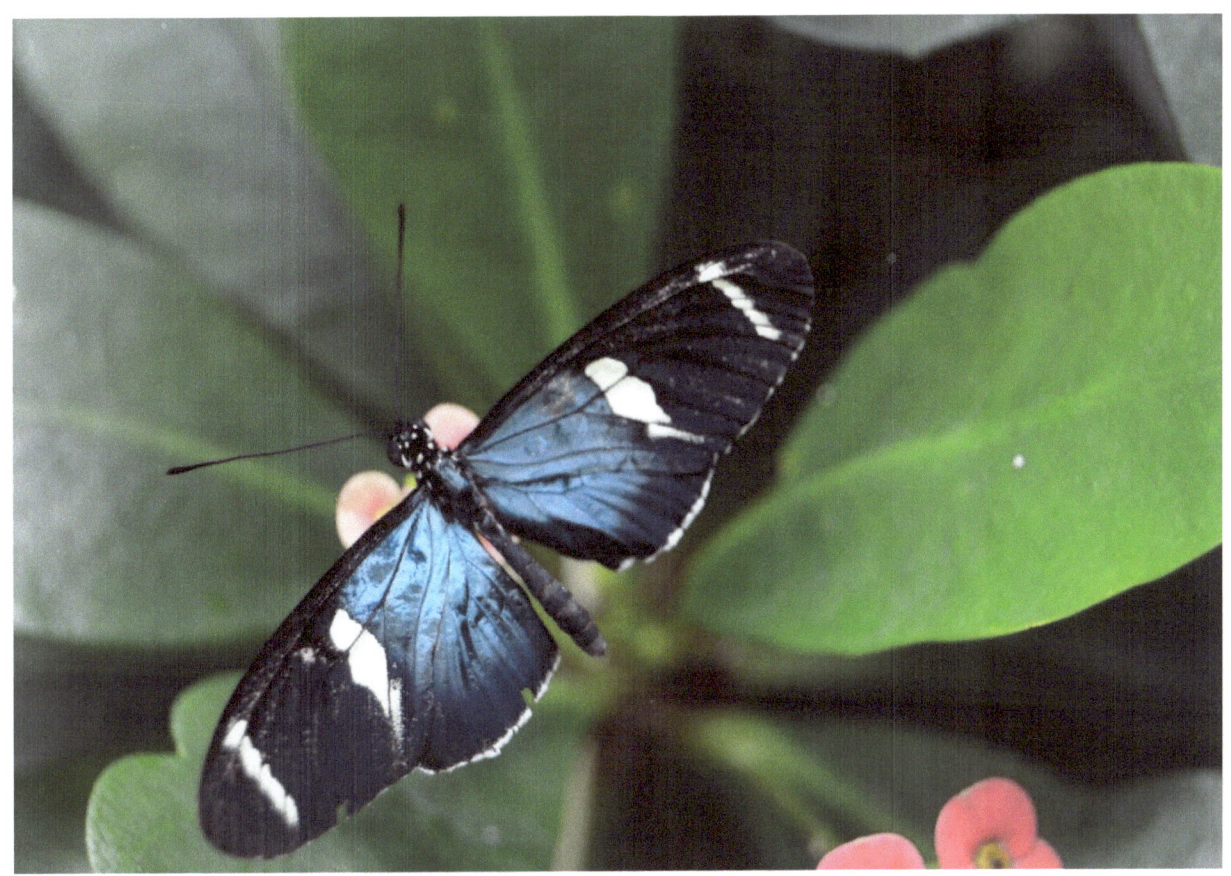

"Gorgeous Blue" Sara Longwing

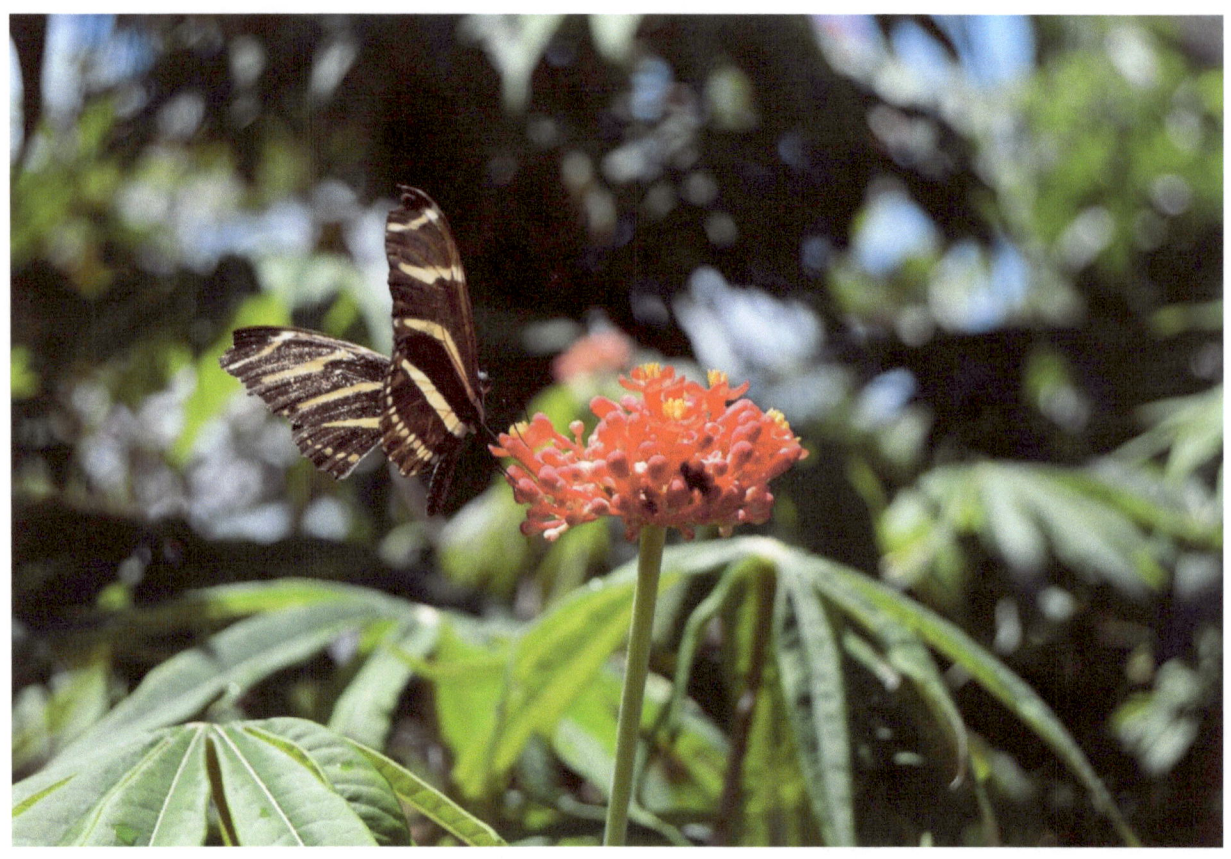

"Greeting Sunrise" Zebra Striped Longwing

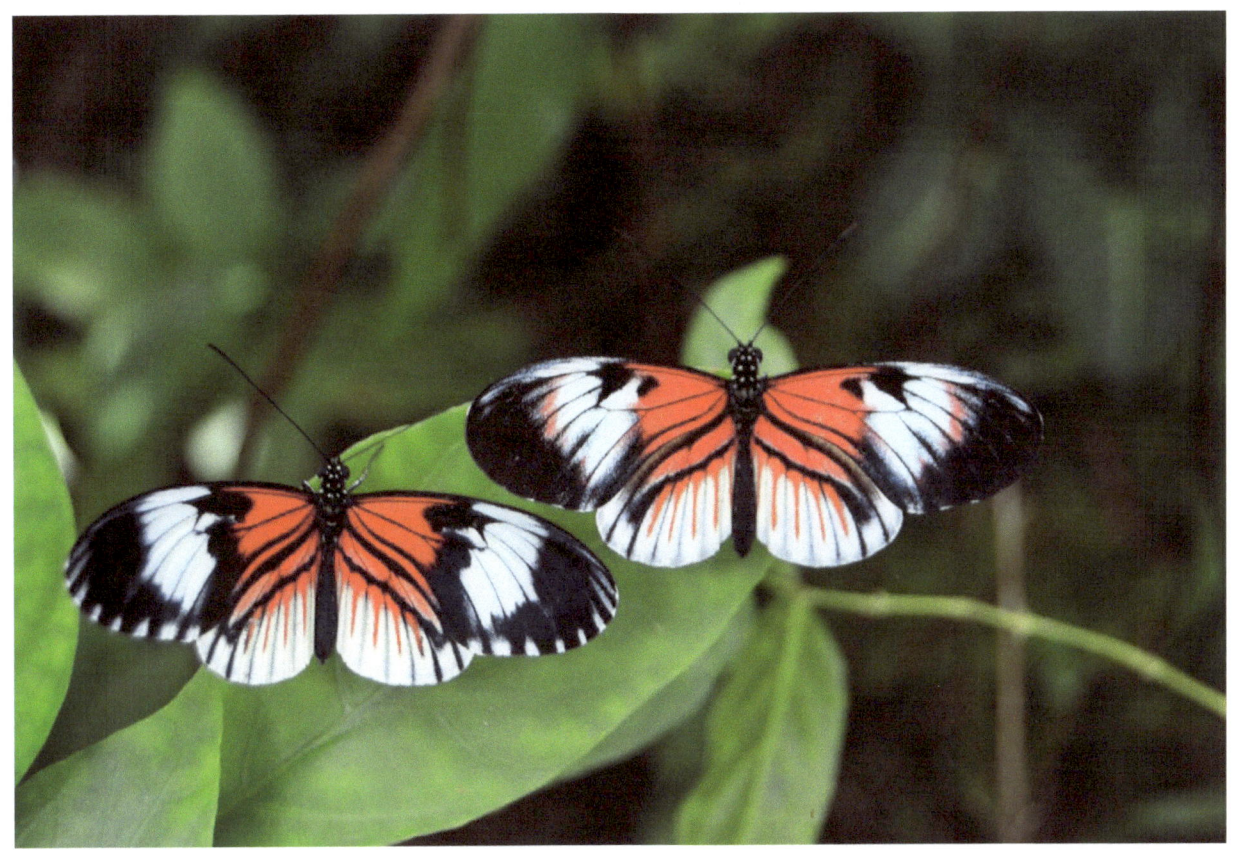

"*The Twins*" Postman

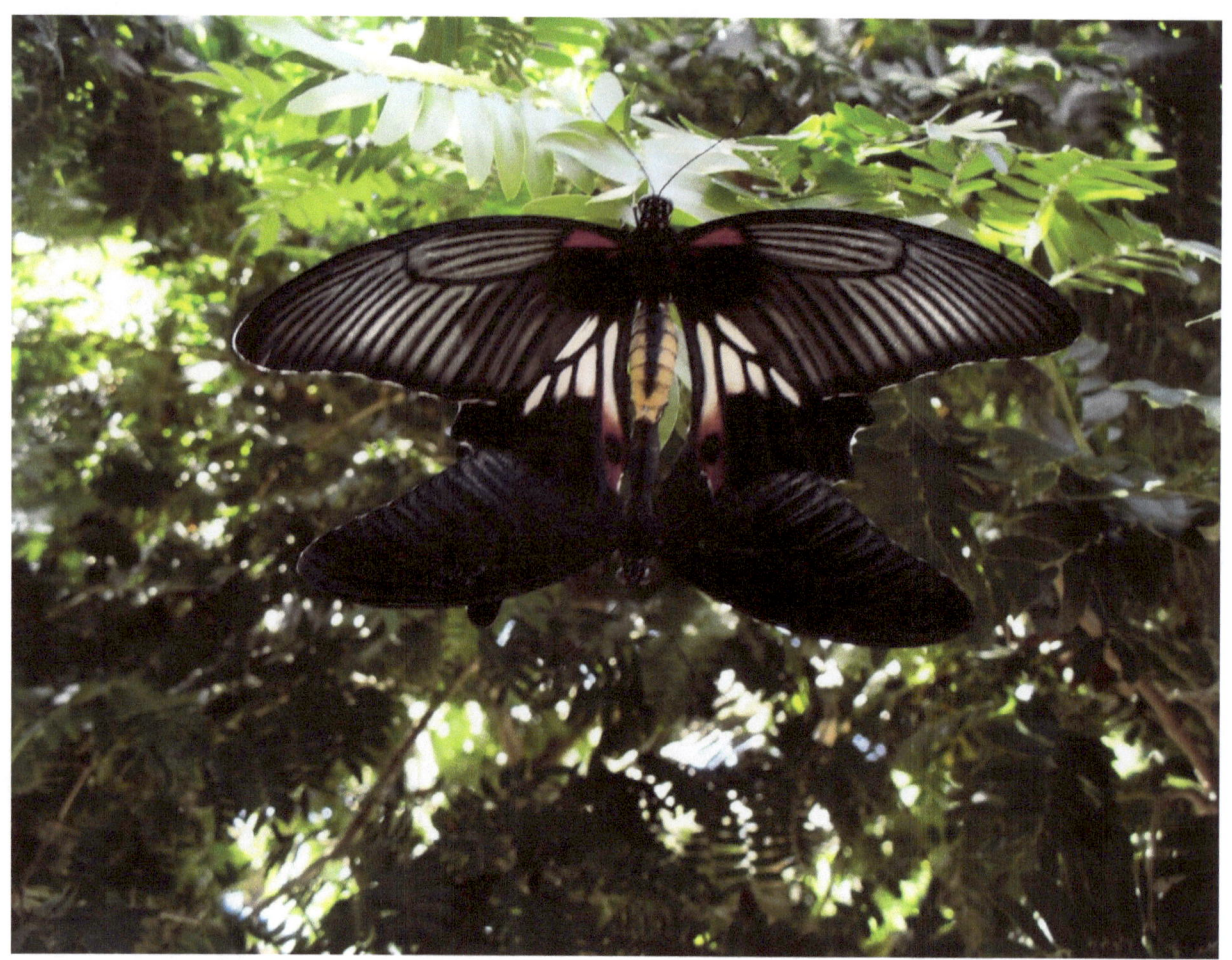

"My Perfect Mate"   The Great Mormons

Notice the female assumes the

dominant position!

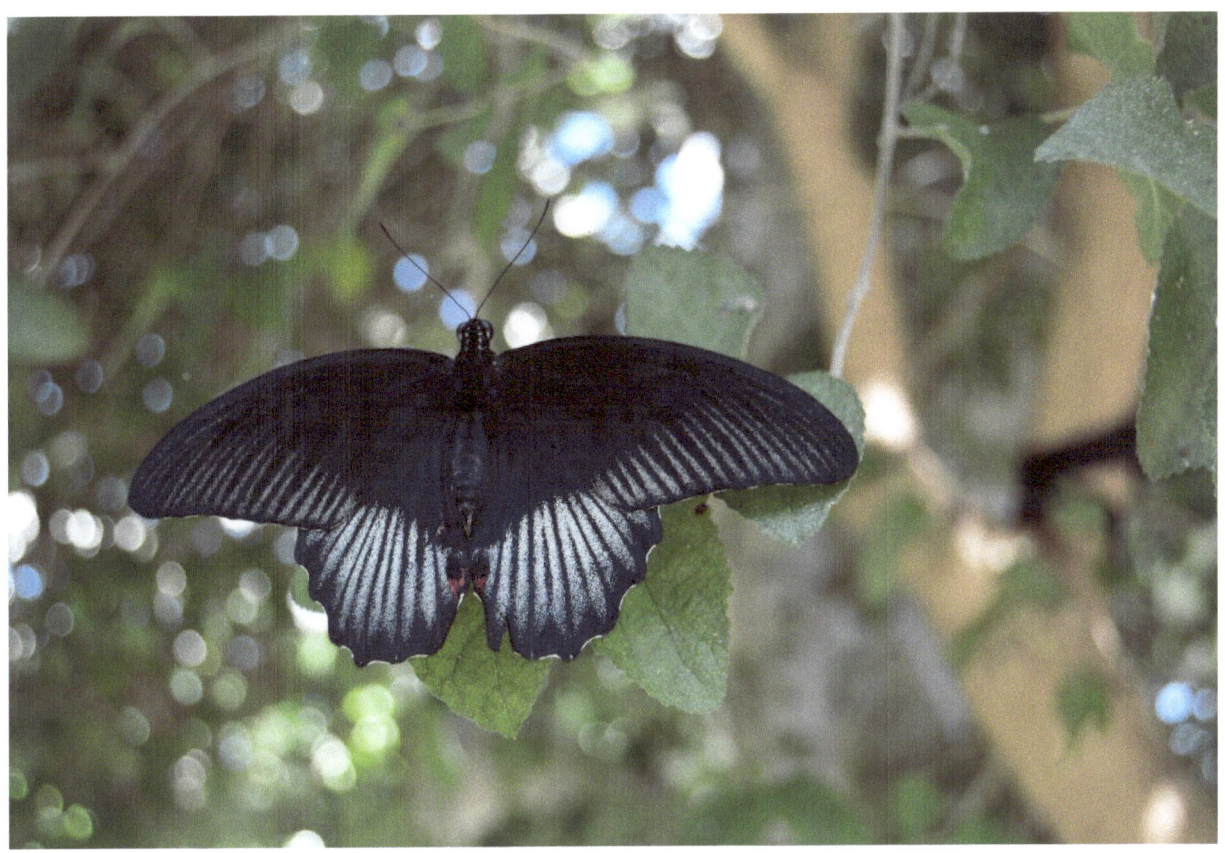

"Black Panther's Sidekick"   Great Mormon male

His majesty ignored my presence,

all together!

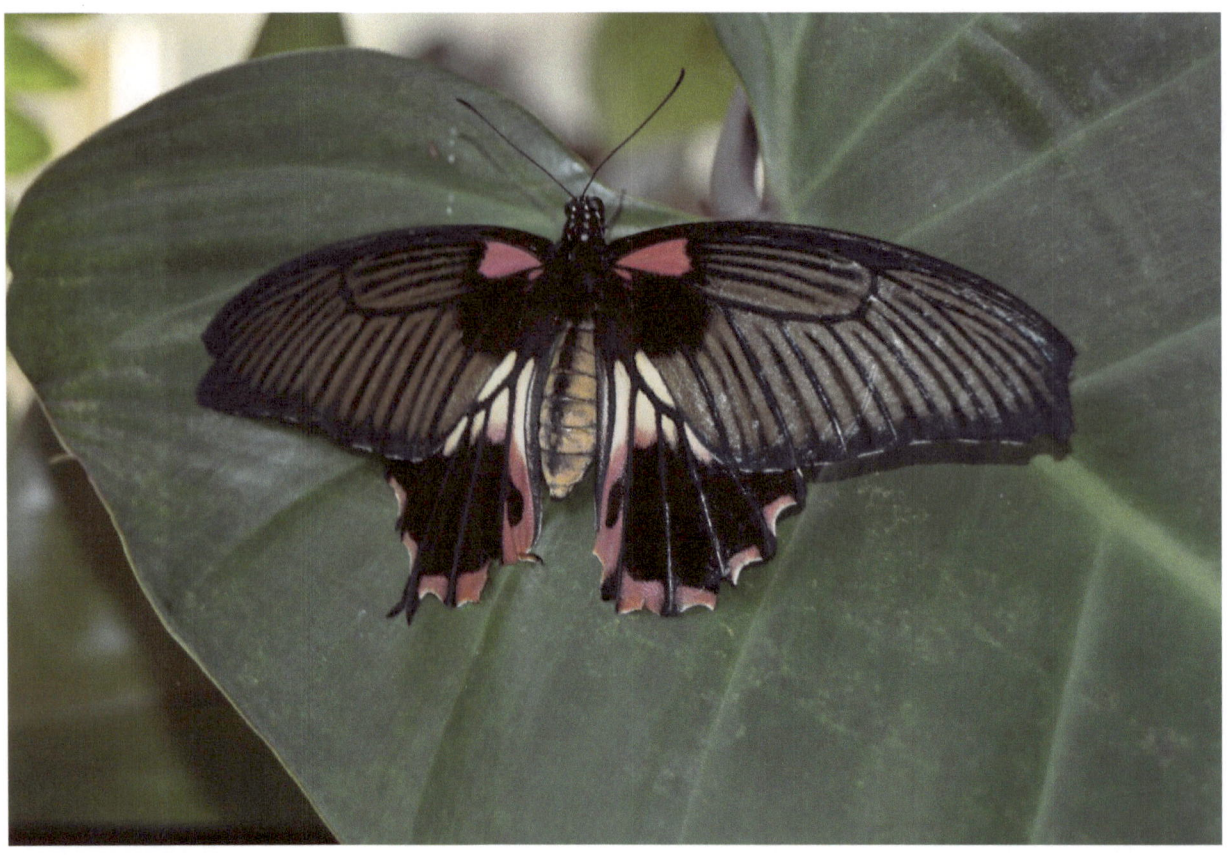

"Pink Lady"　　　　　　　　　　　　　　　　　　Great Mormon Female

Notice again, most often the
ladies bring the bling!

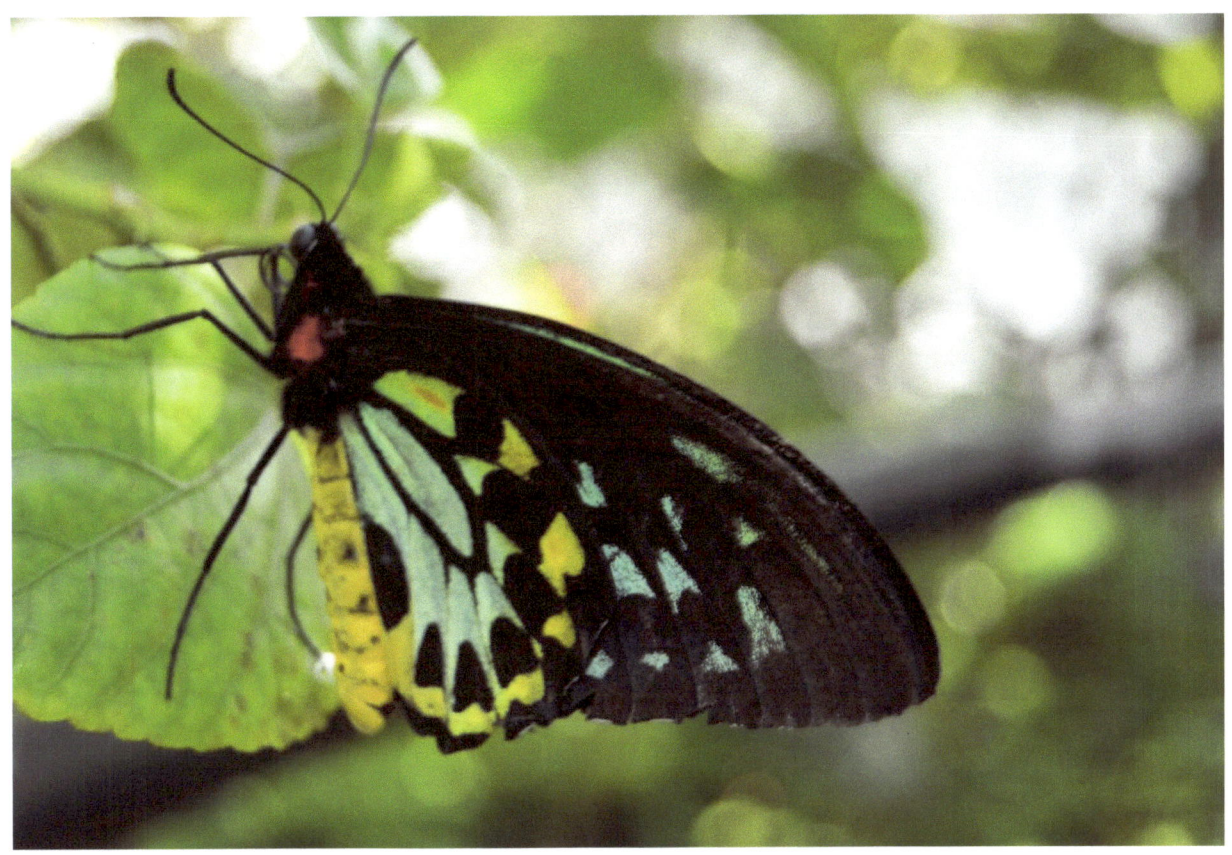

"Always Bring Beauty"   Golden Birdwing

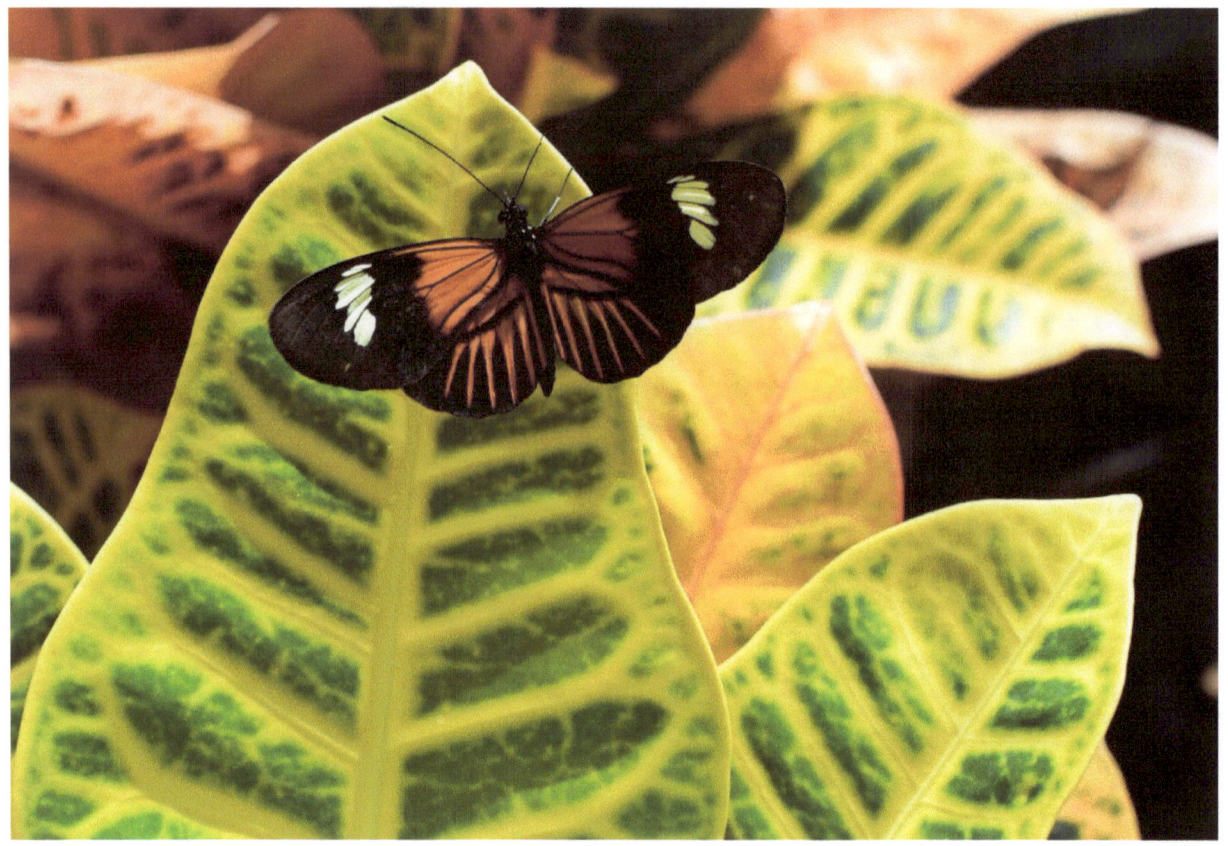

"Morning Glory" #3   Doris Longwing

These colorful creatures love to find places to camouflage themselves!

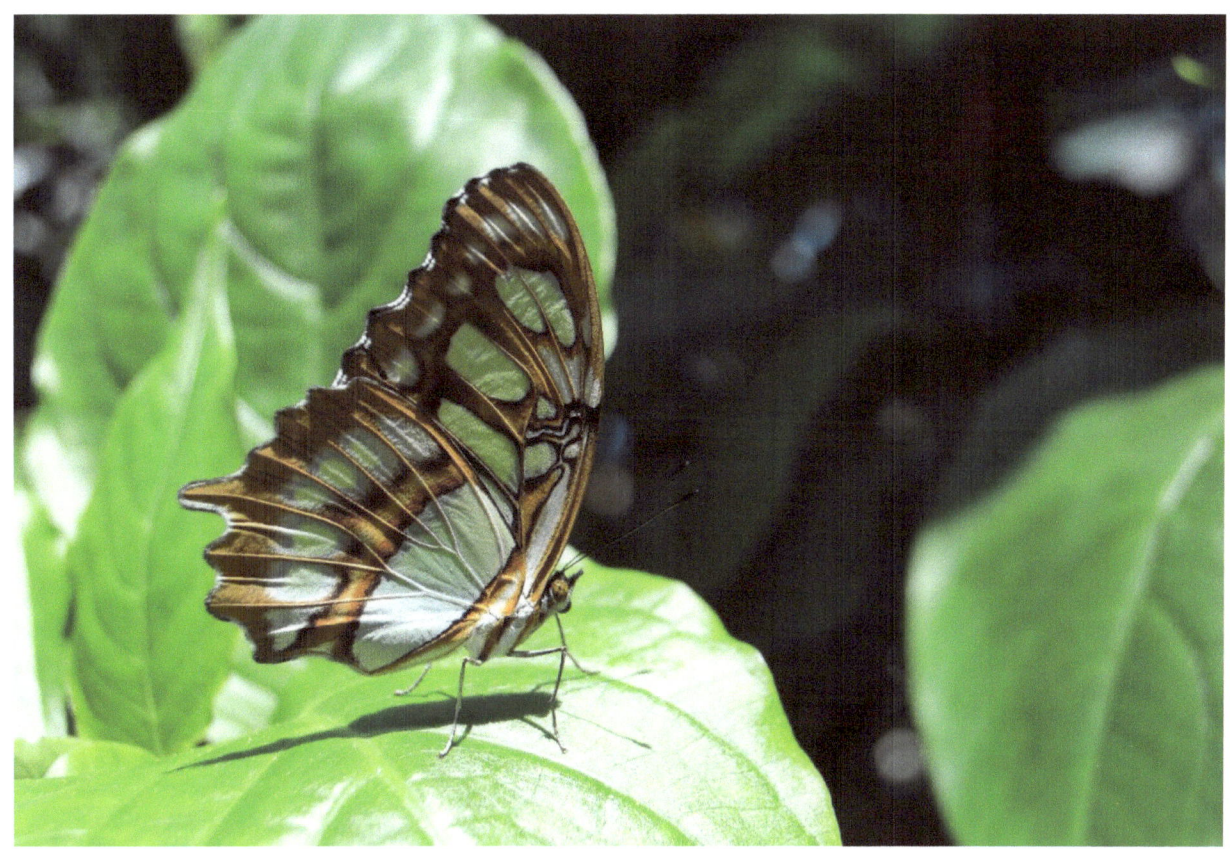

"*Memories of Emmett*" Malachite

Notice the beautiful brown eye which

matches the brown of its wings

More Than Surviving . . . Thriving

In past years, while preparing for exhibitions, I always tried to select the most 'perfect' specimens (wings intact, without damage or blemishes). But what I realize now is that they, like all of us, do not have perfect bodies, mine certainly is not!

My photographs show butterflies soaring gardens and skies without limitations, though sometimes missing parts of their wings, or growing old. As I said previously, shamelessly presenting their beauty for all the world to see is all they do continuously. They do not compare themselves to or imitate other creatures. They effortlessly bring beauty wherever they go. They continue not just surviving but thriving. They live their fullest, most glamorous life despite sometimes having scars or wounds! This is a powerful lesson for us!

For many years of my nursing career, I worked with people who are differently abled. Like the variety and diversity of butterflies, (and all of us), their lives have meaning and serve purpose in this world. We all have in common the desire to be loved, accepted, connected, and to contribute meaningfully to the world around us. We learn this lesson too from the butterflies!

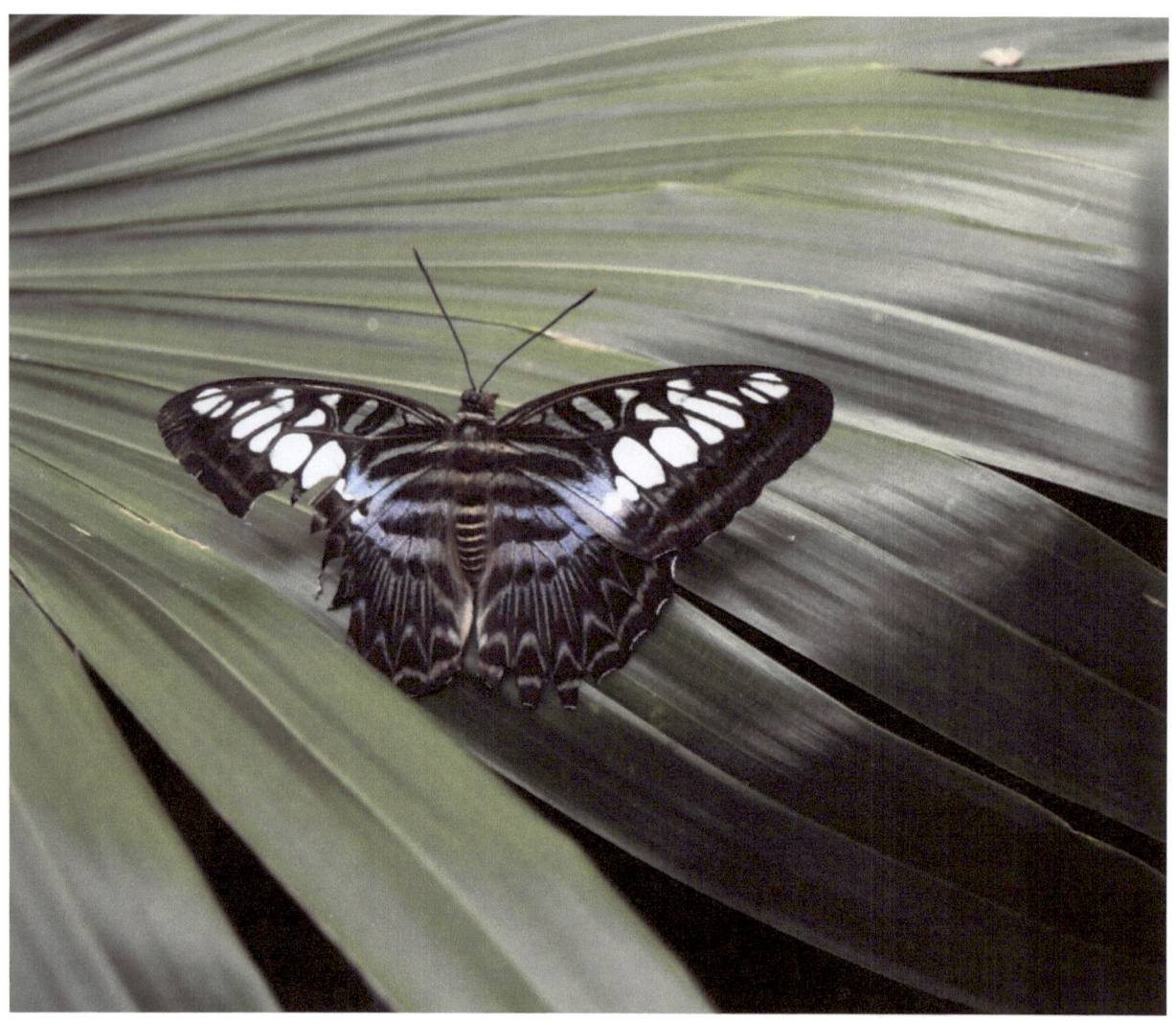

"Survivor"   Brown Clipper

Moving forward continuously!

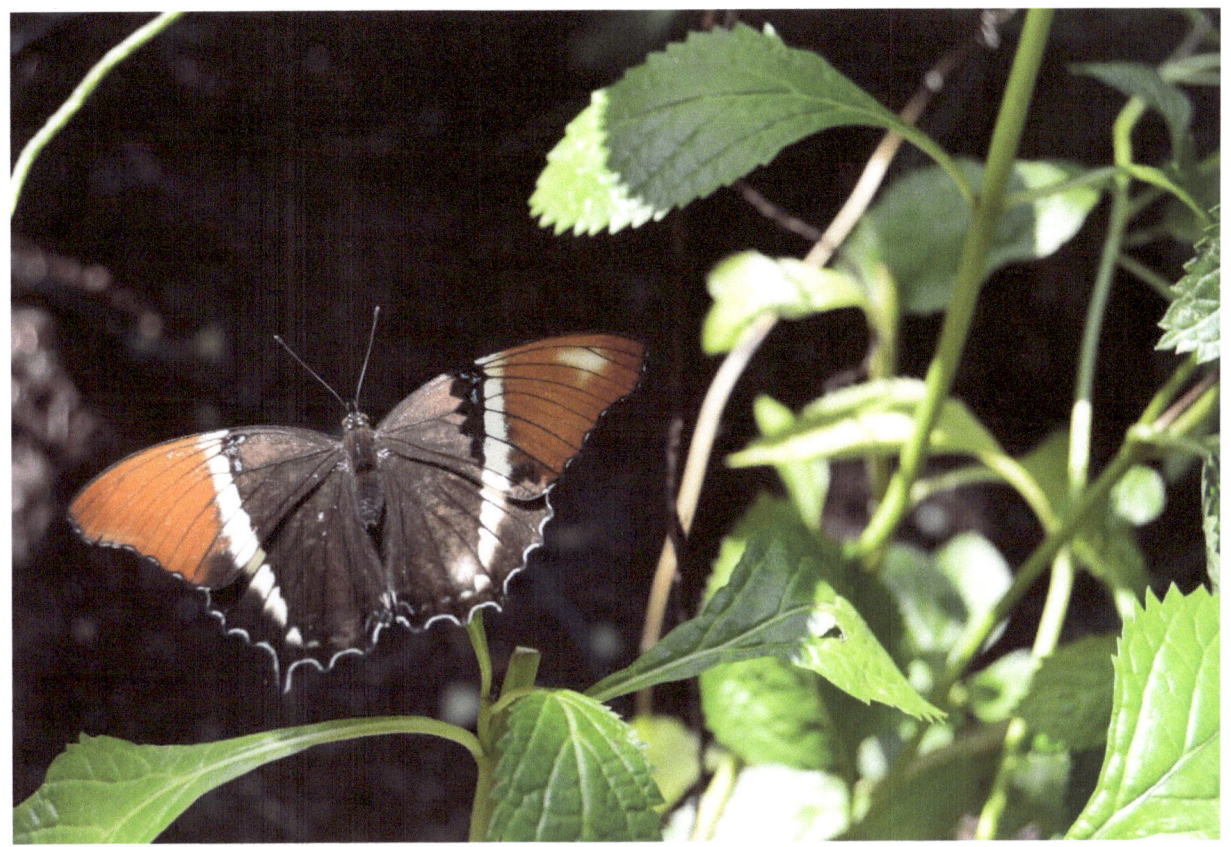

"Aging Well" Rusty-tipped Page

Continuous grace & beauty!

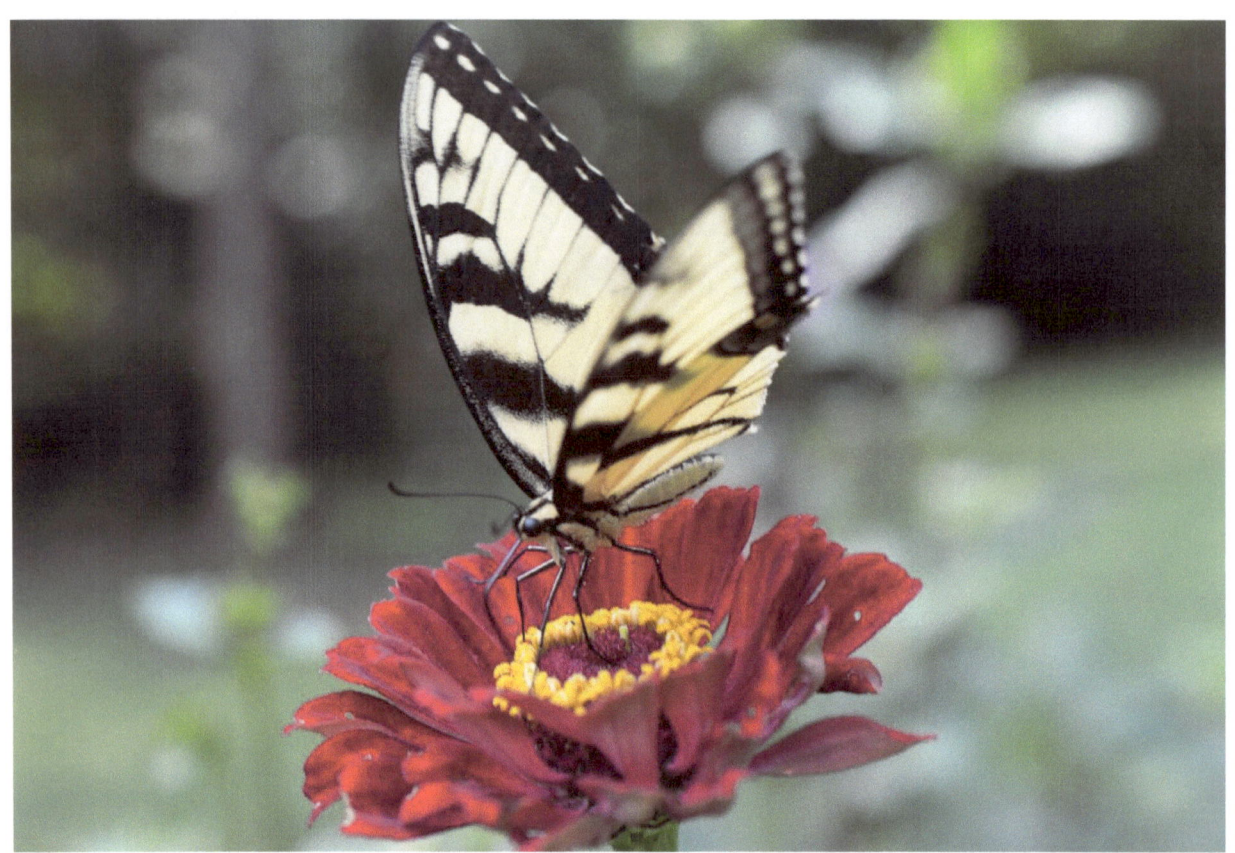

"Great Escape"   Tiger Swallowtail

Capturing this beauty in my back yard,

I am sure it was almost a bird's dinner!

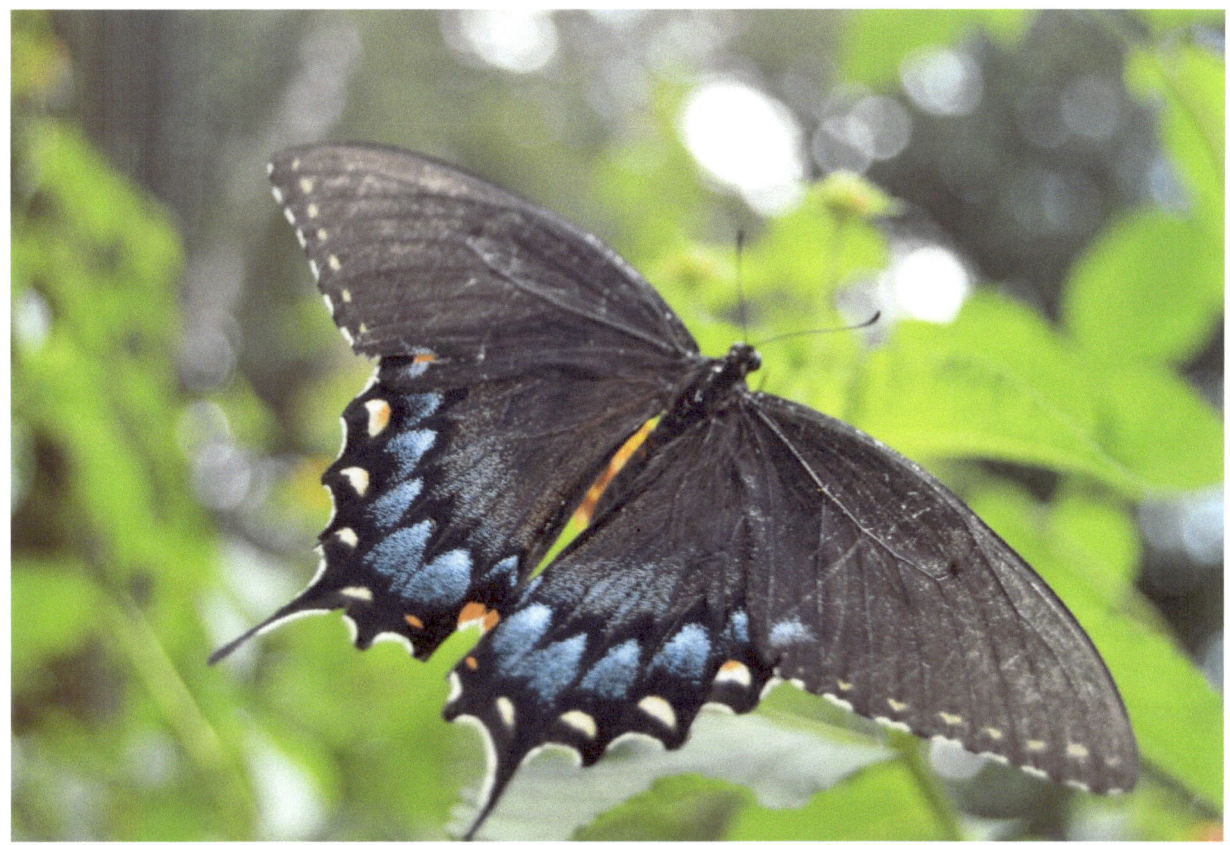

"*Ageless Beauty*" Black Swallowtail

As they age, butterflies, like all of us

begin to lose texture and color

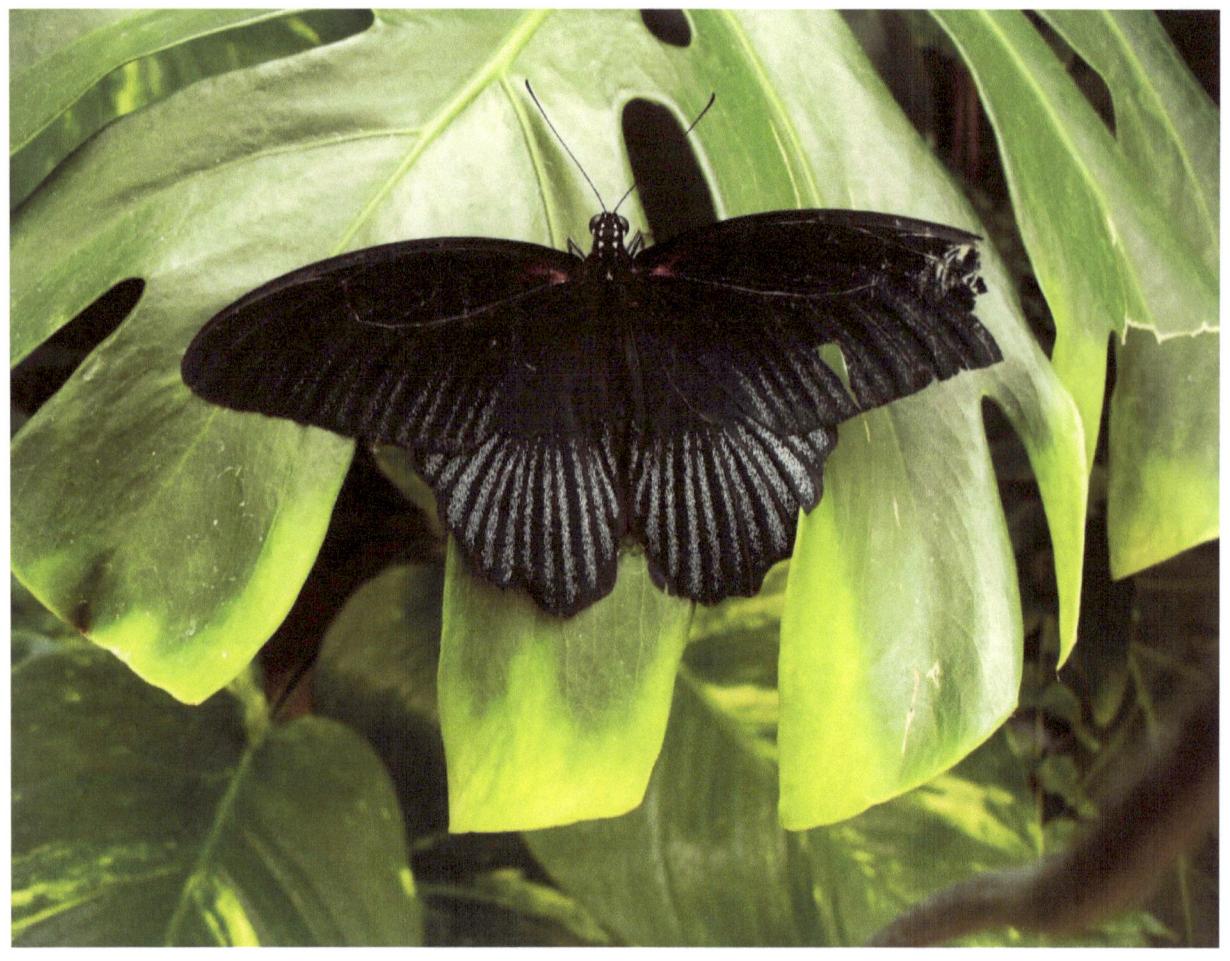

"More Than Surviving"   Great Mormon

Fulfilling his purpose beautifully!

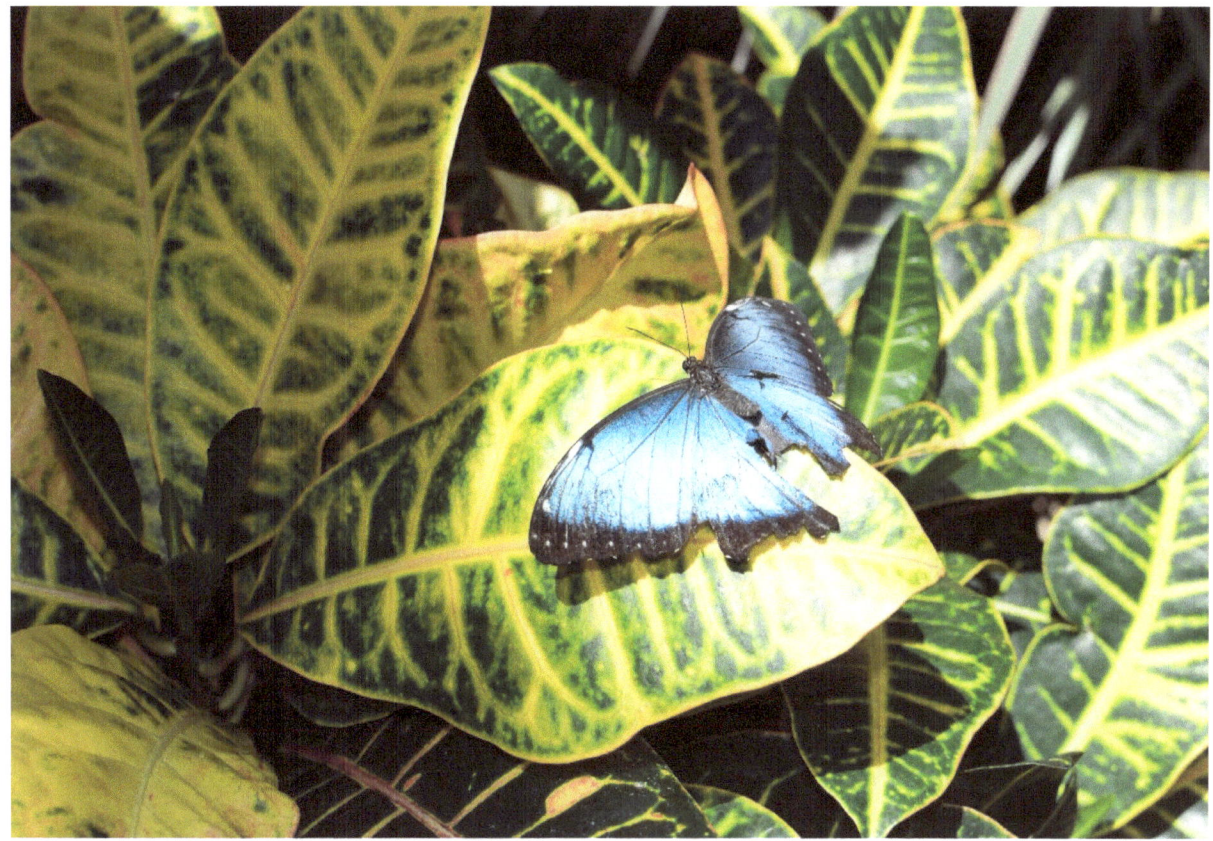

"Still Keeping On" Blue Morpho

Taking a rest in the sun!

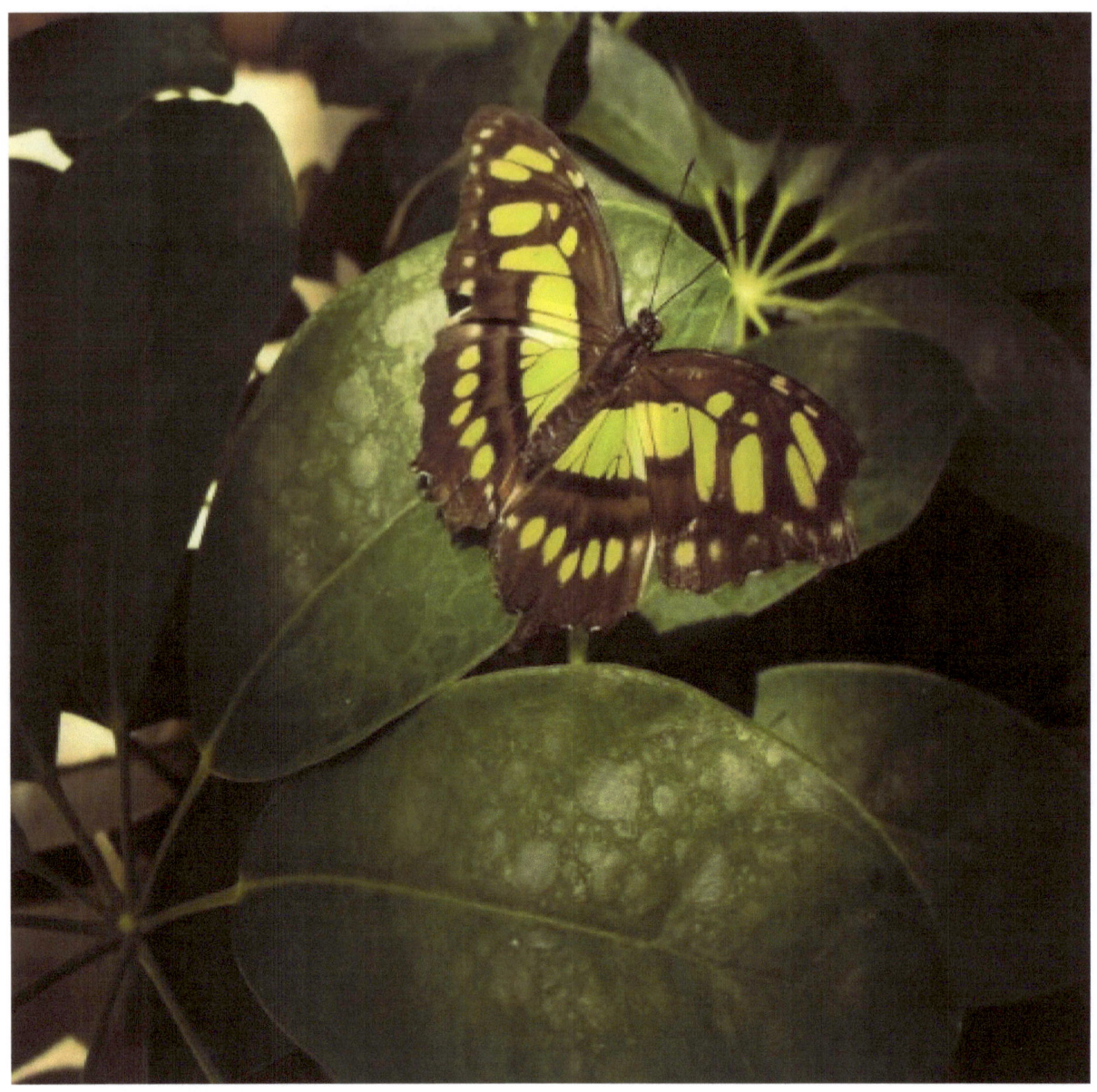

"I've Known Rivers"   Malachite

They calmly go with the flow always!

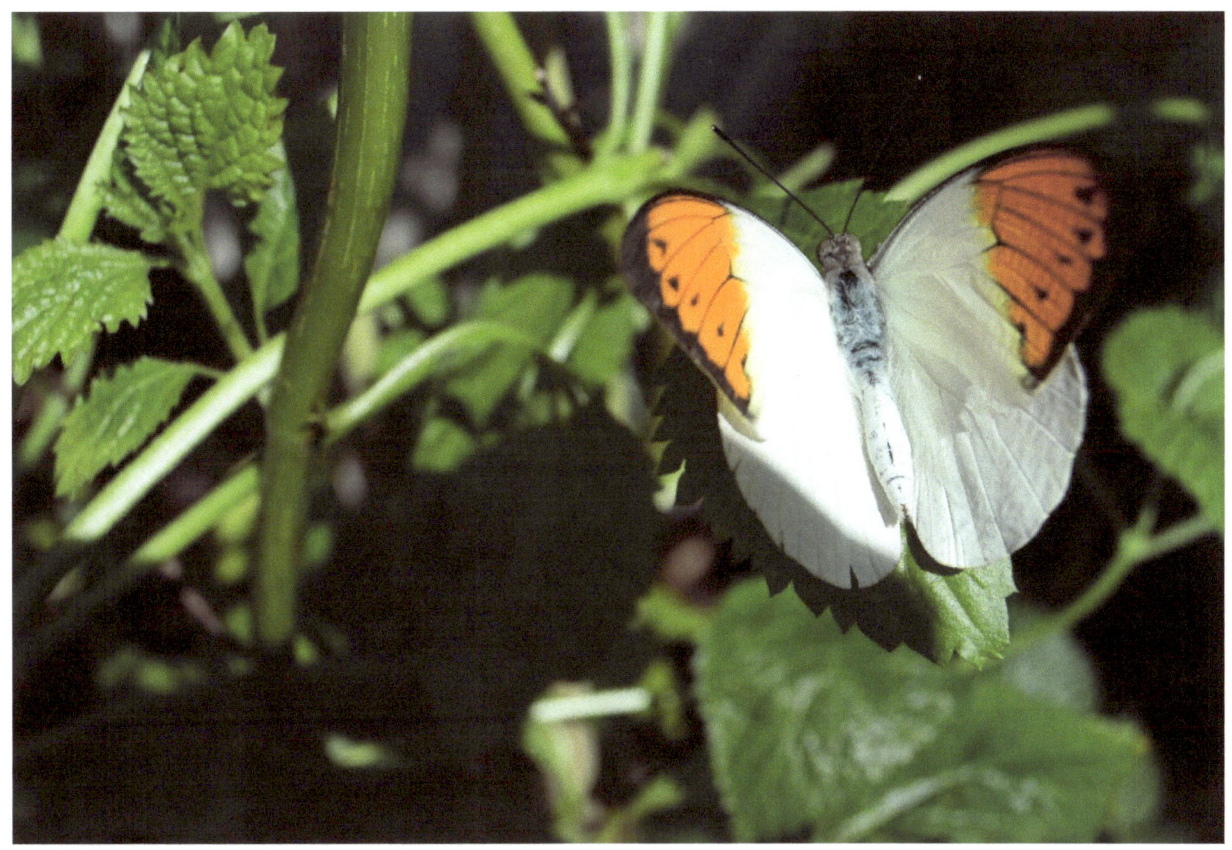

"Seen Many Days" Great Orange Tip

They keep going, beauty in movement

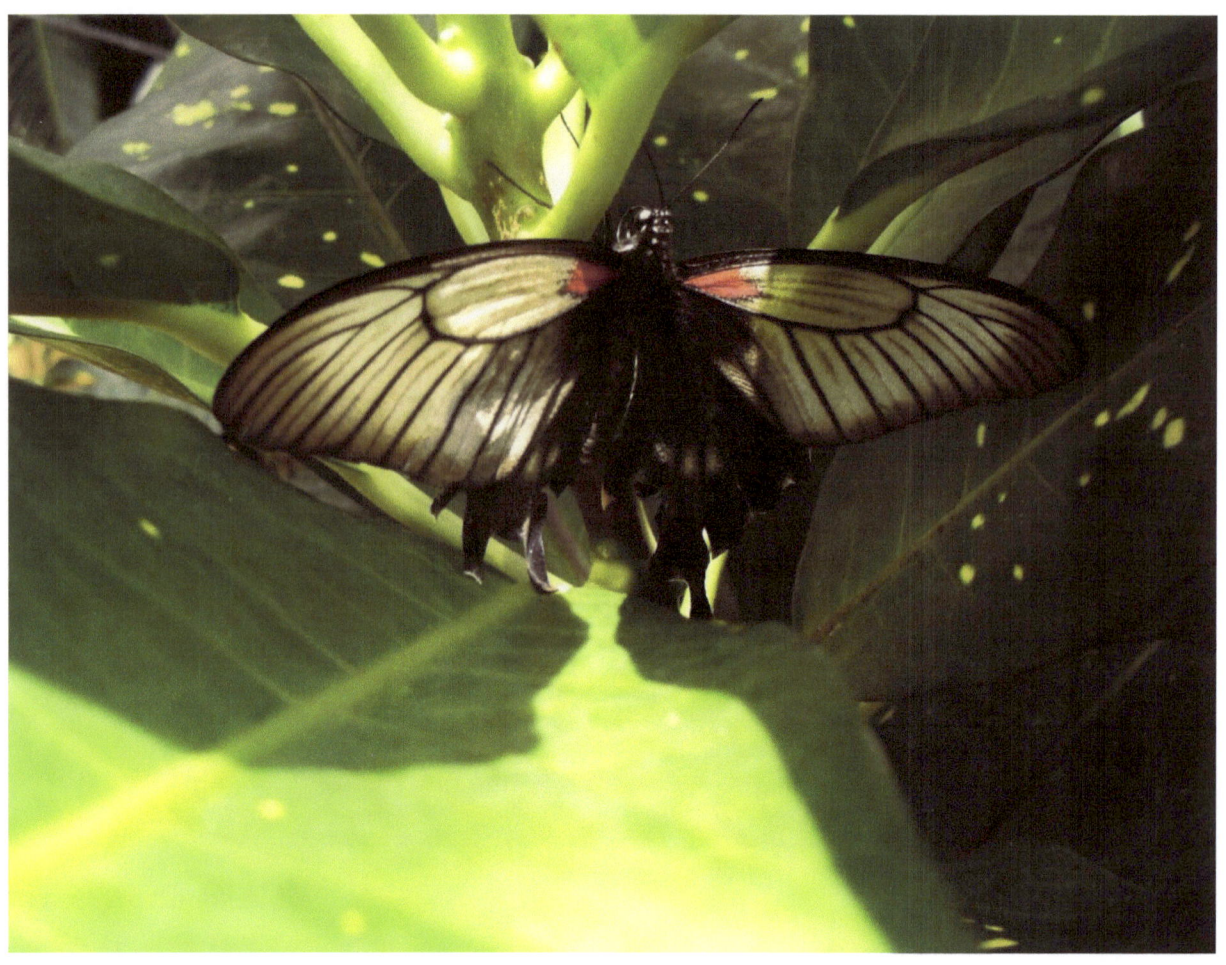

"Rest in Peace" Great Mormon Swallowtail

This beauty found her final

resting place in sun light among the leaves

"Like the Butterflies: Go Wherever You Please & Please Wherever you Go!"

This saying is carved on a bench at Butterfly World. It was an homage to the beautiful creatures of all sizes and colors flying around it. It encourages us again to always bring beauty. The sudden, unexpected arrival of a butterfly brings delight to most everyone. I have heard people say these joyful creatures arrived at times when they were experiencing sorrow or sadness, such as at a graveside. Perhaps they were experiencing despair or grief, when suddenly, out of nowhere, they were able to experience joy and hope when they were joined by one of these beauties. Their presence is always fascinating and delightful!

In April of this year, I had an opportunity to visit my family in Florida. Of course we took the smallest ones to Butterfly World. I found however, that the little ones were apprehensive around live butterflies, having not been up close before. My five-year-old granddaughter was fortunate enough to spend time with some other little girls her age, who were fearless around them! One of the little girls approached her with an exotic beauty on her finger. She then gently placed it on my granddaughter's finger, dispelling all her fears. The scene reminded me of how these creatures can bring peace and tranquility to most every situation. My granddaughter now views them in a new light. She began extending her finger and smiling brightly, once finding that she could do the same thing!

Finally, I see these creatures as a reminder of what is peaceful, delightful, and mysterious in our world. They remind us that we too can bring beauty, calmness, and peace wherever we go! Listen to the butterflies, they speak wisdom and joy!

I hope you enjoy this collection as much as I have putting it together! I believe now my grandmother would be proud. I don't need jars anymore!

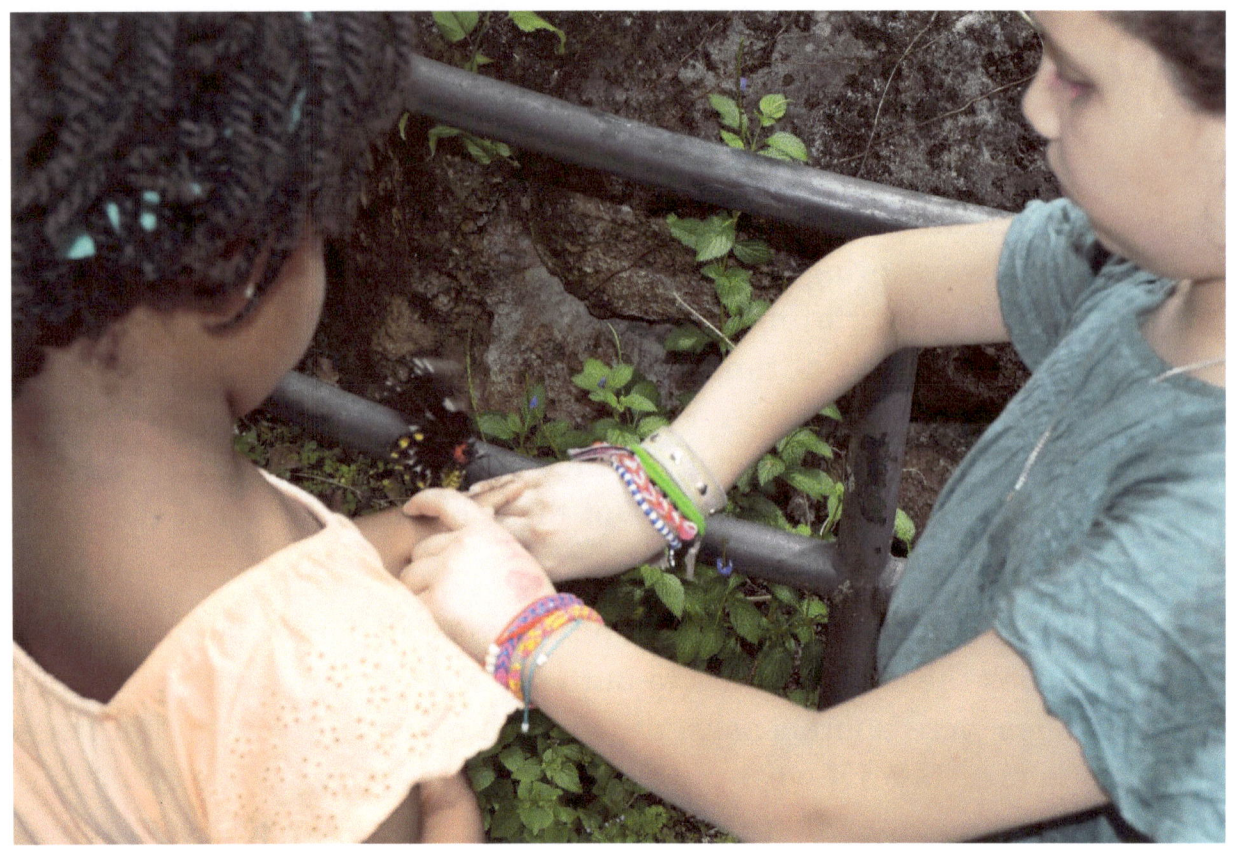

"Let's be Friends"   Golden Birdwing

One picture is worth a thousand words!

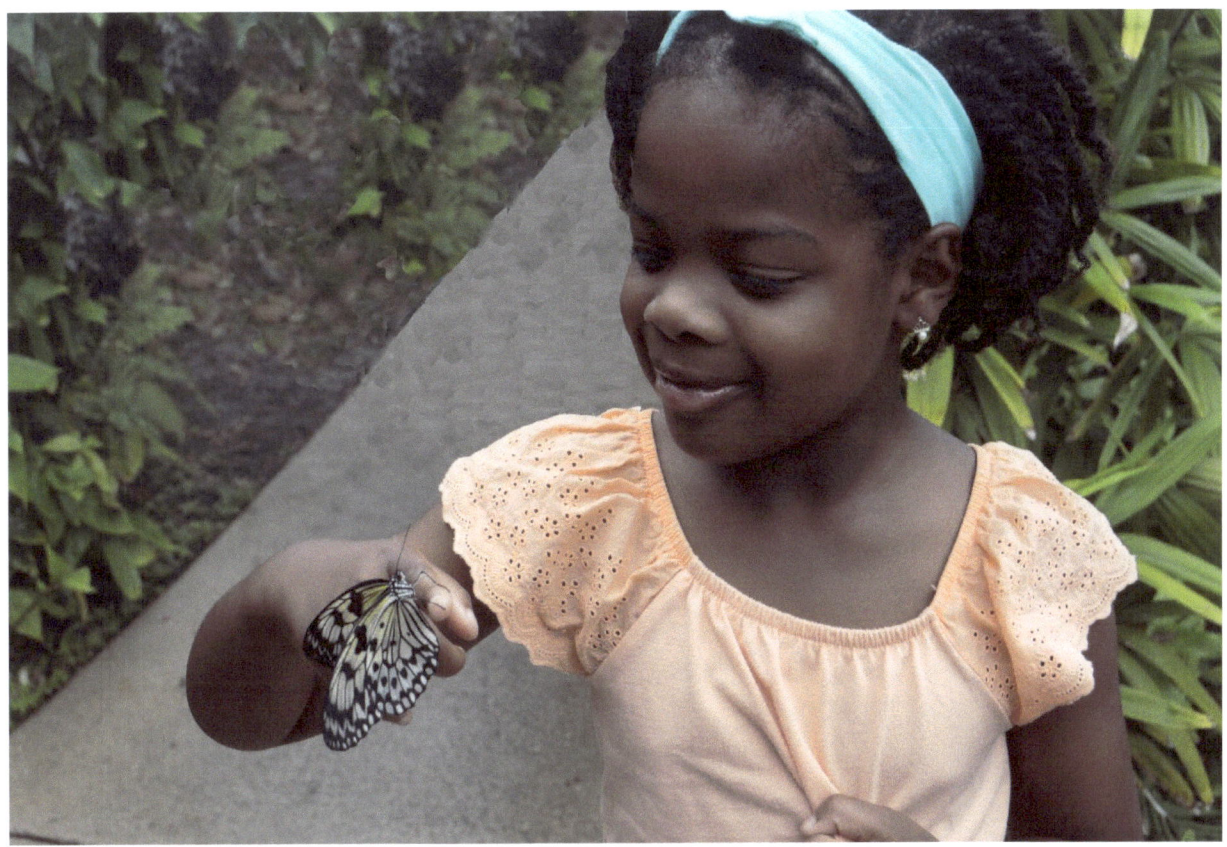

"My New Friend" Rice Paper

For the rest of the afternoon, she smiled and reminisced about her new adventure!

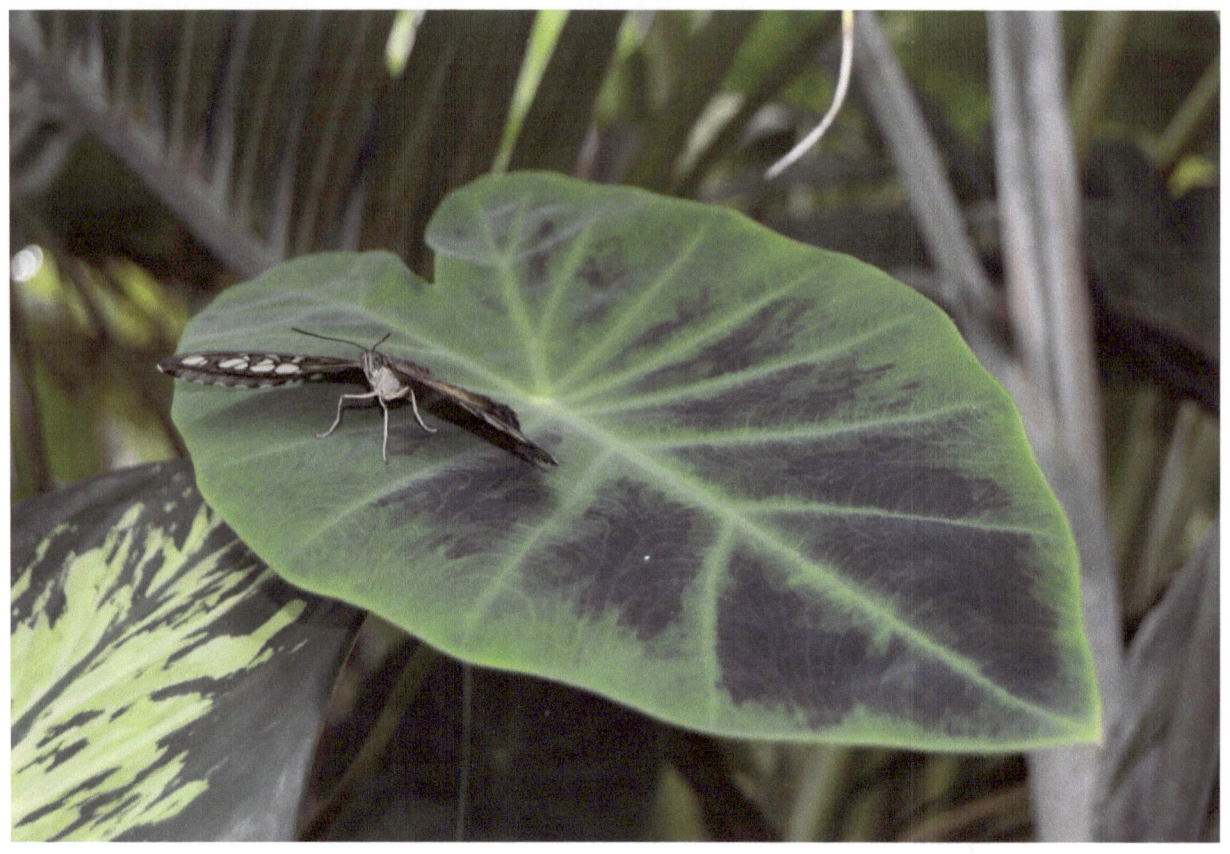

"Landing Pad" Brown Clipper

I noticed this beauty suddenly,

it seemed waiting for me to notice it

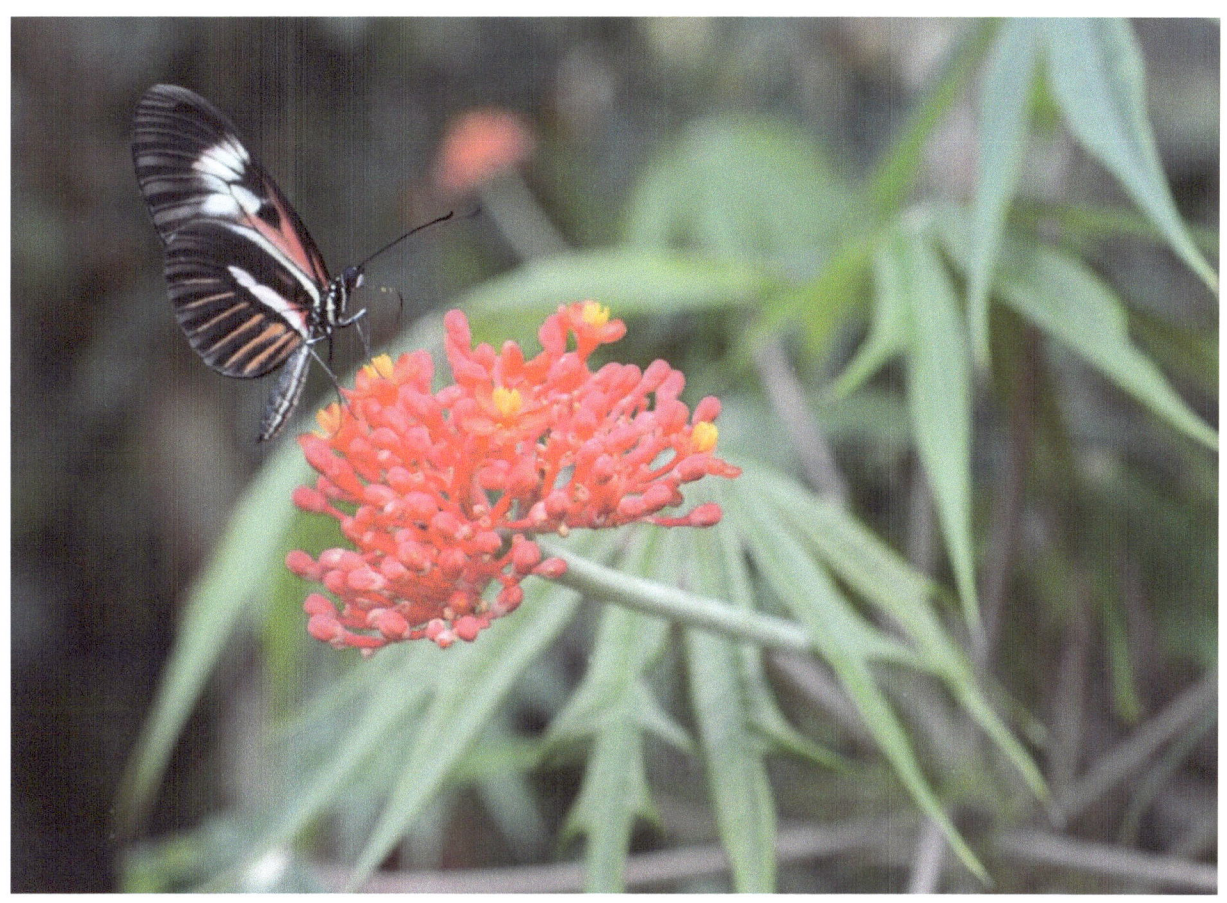

"Sitting Pretty" #2   Brush Footed

Again, ignoring our presence,

they go about meeting their needs

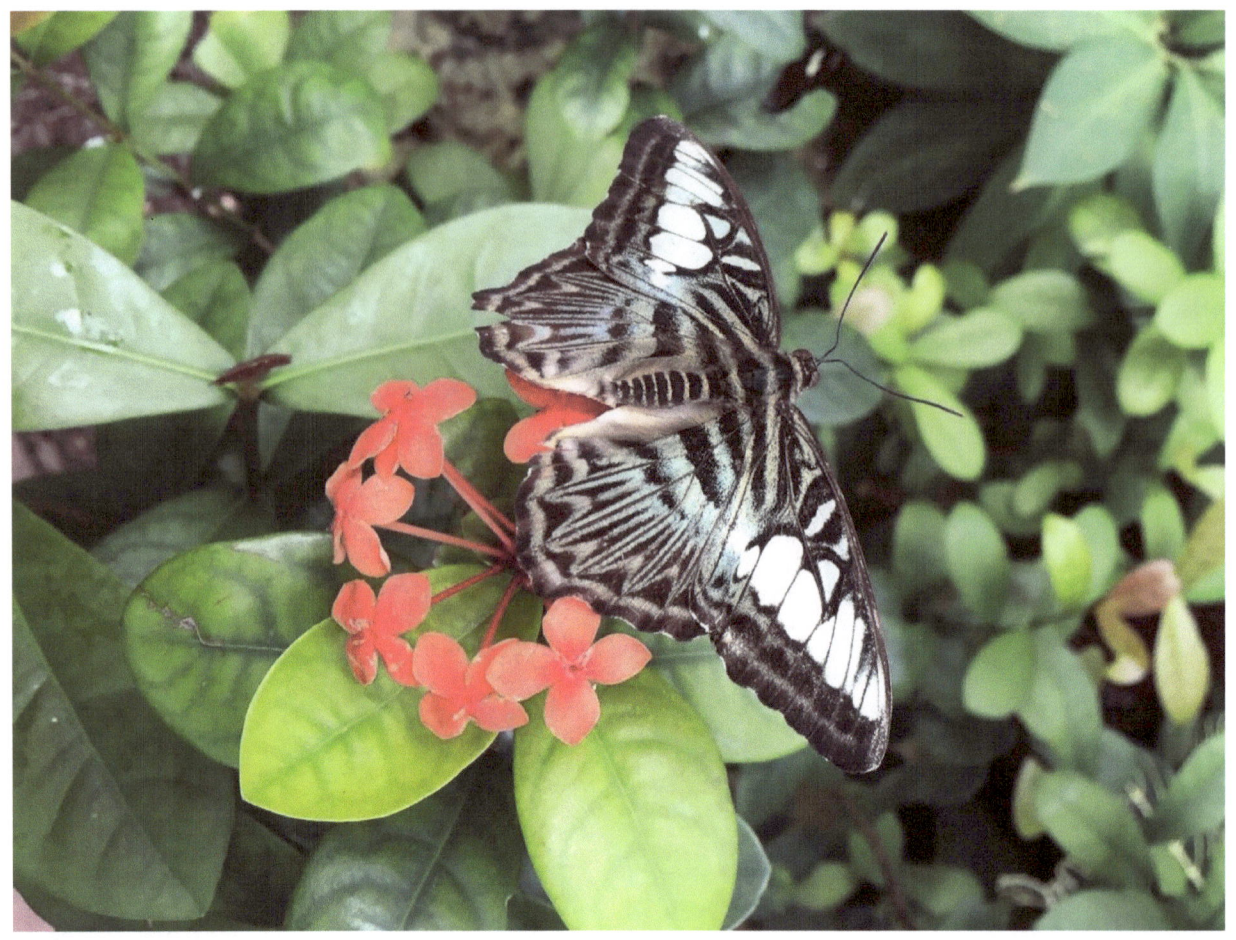

"*Brown Beauty*"   Brown Clipper

Another one that camouflages well!

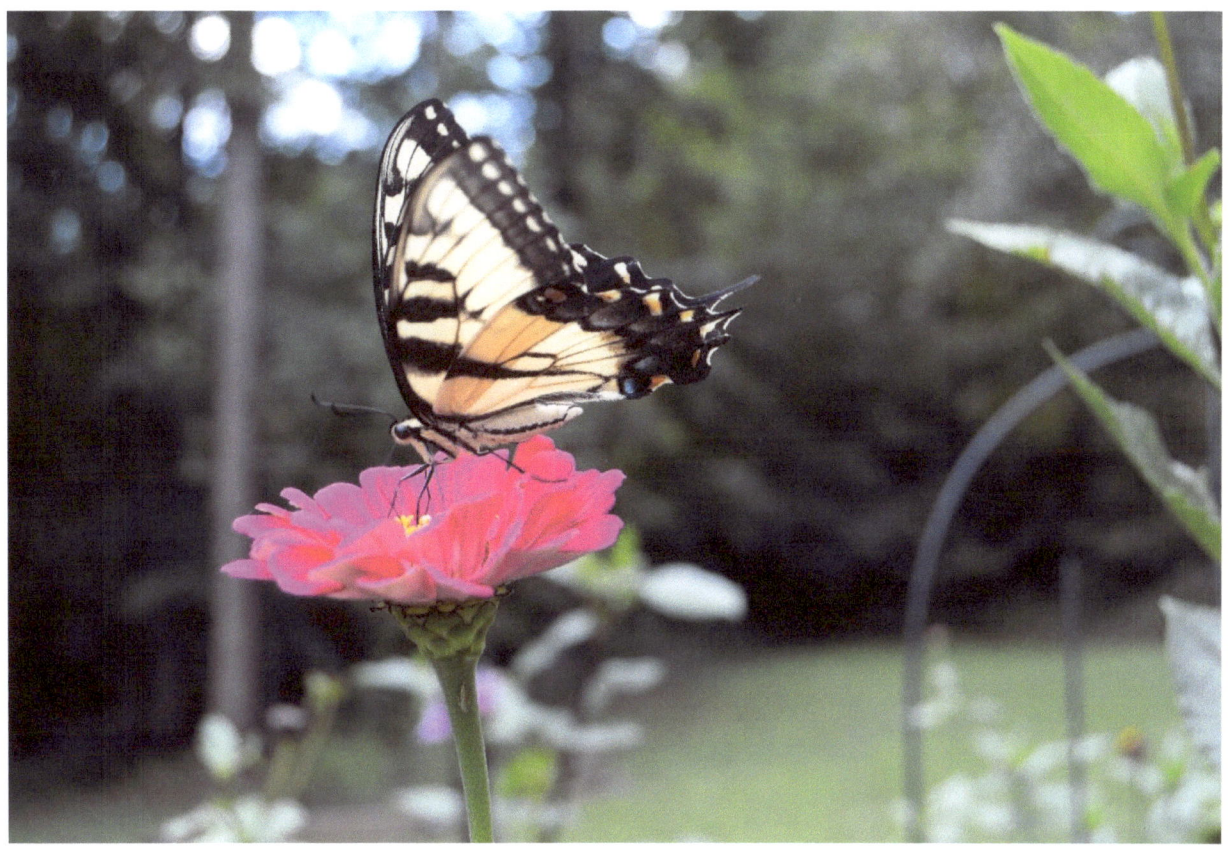

"Snack Time" Tiger Swallowtail

Gorgeous delight in my back yard!

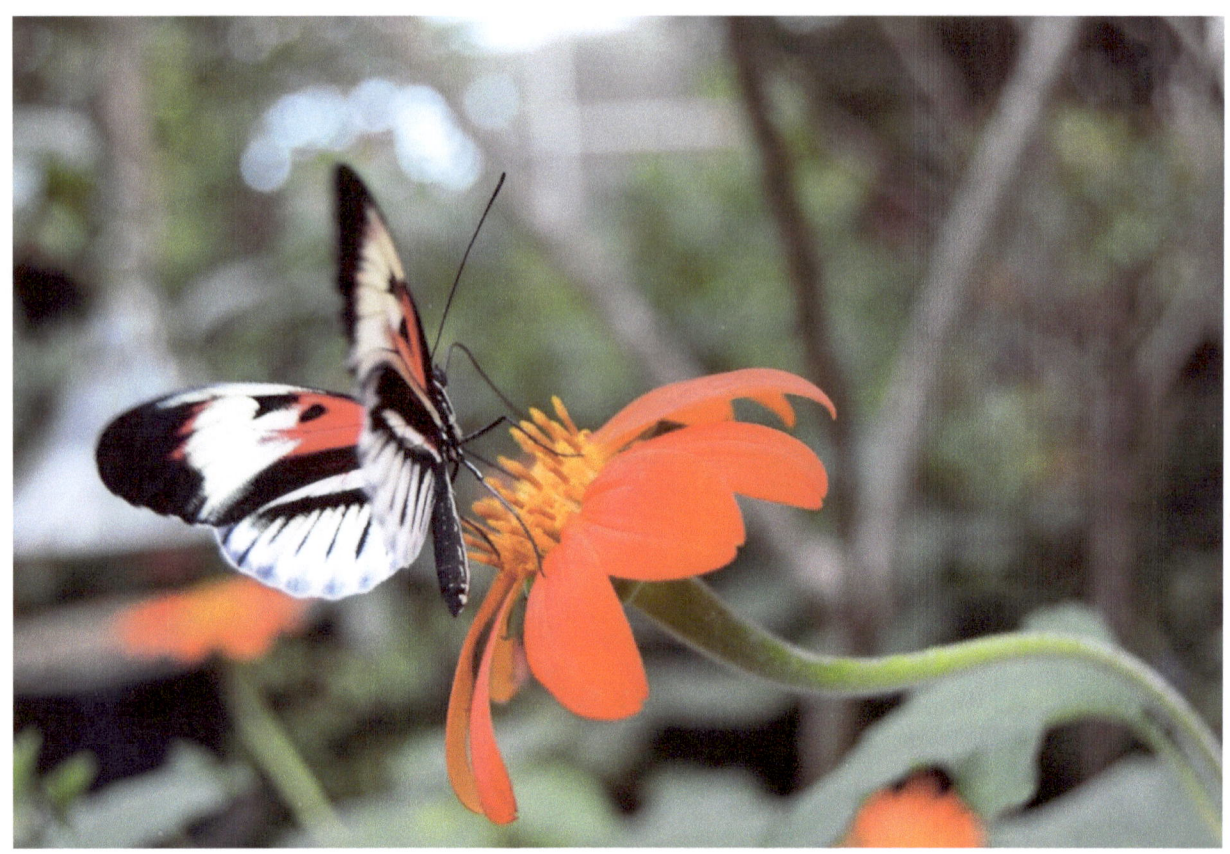

"Breakfast Break"   Postman

The Postman seems to love

orange flowers!

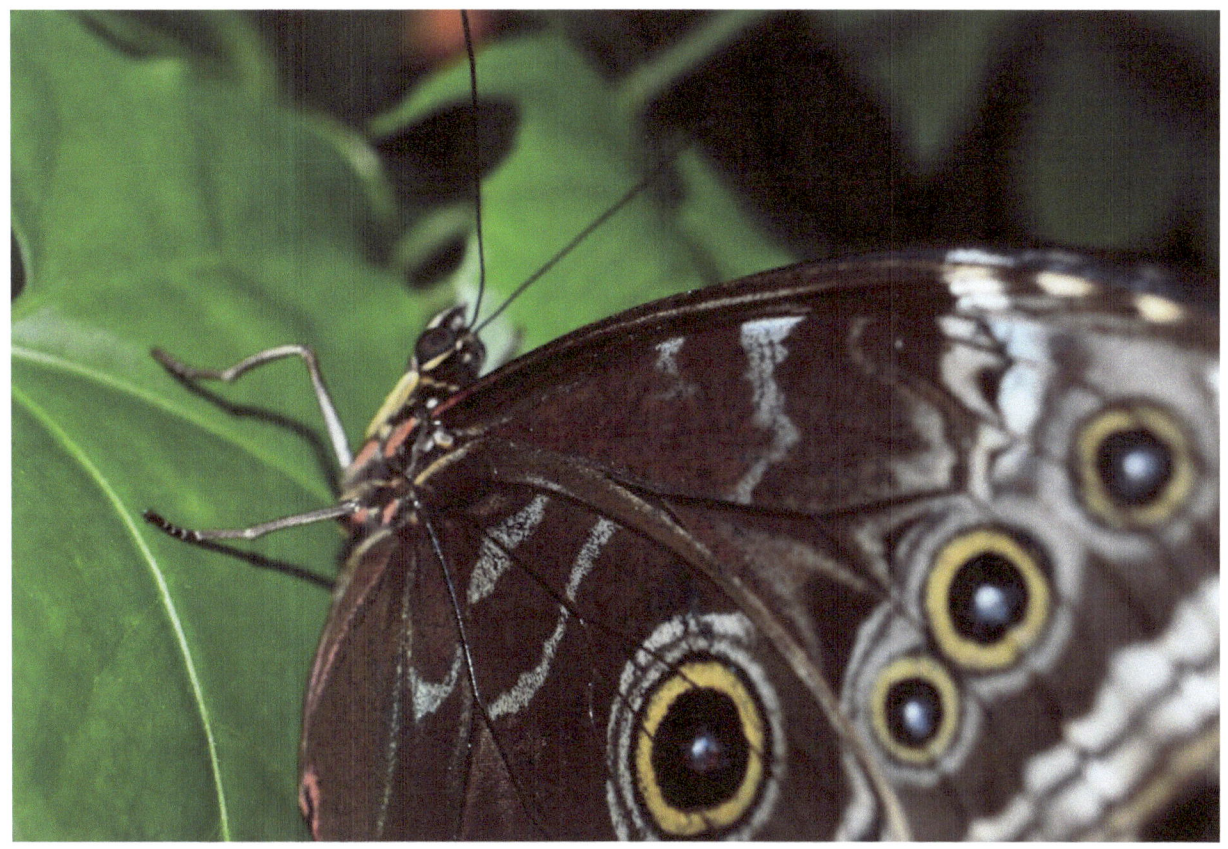

"Old Blue Eyes" #4   Blue Morpho

One of my absolute favorites!

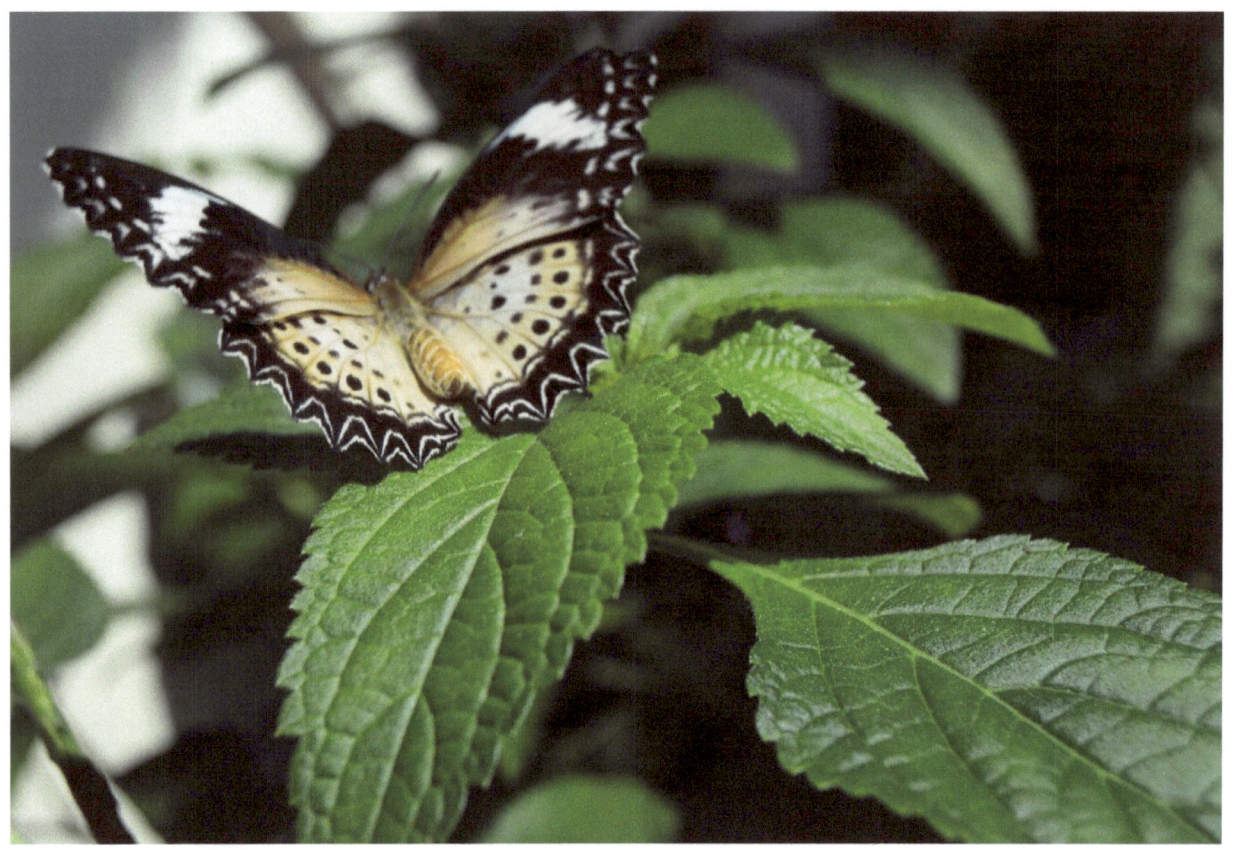

"Right At Home"   Leopard Lacewing

Named appropriately for its

stunning lace wing pattern!

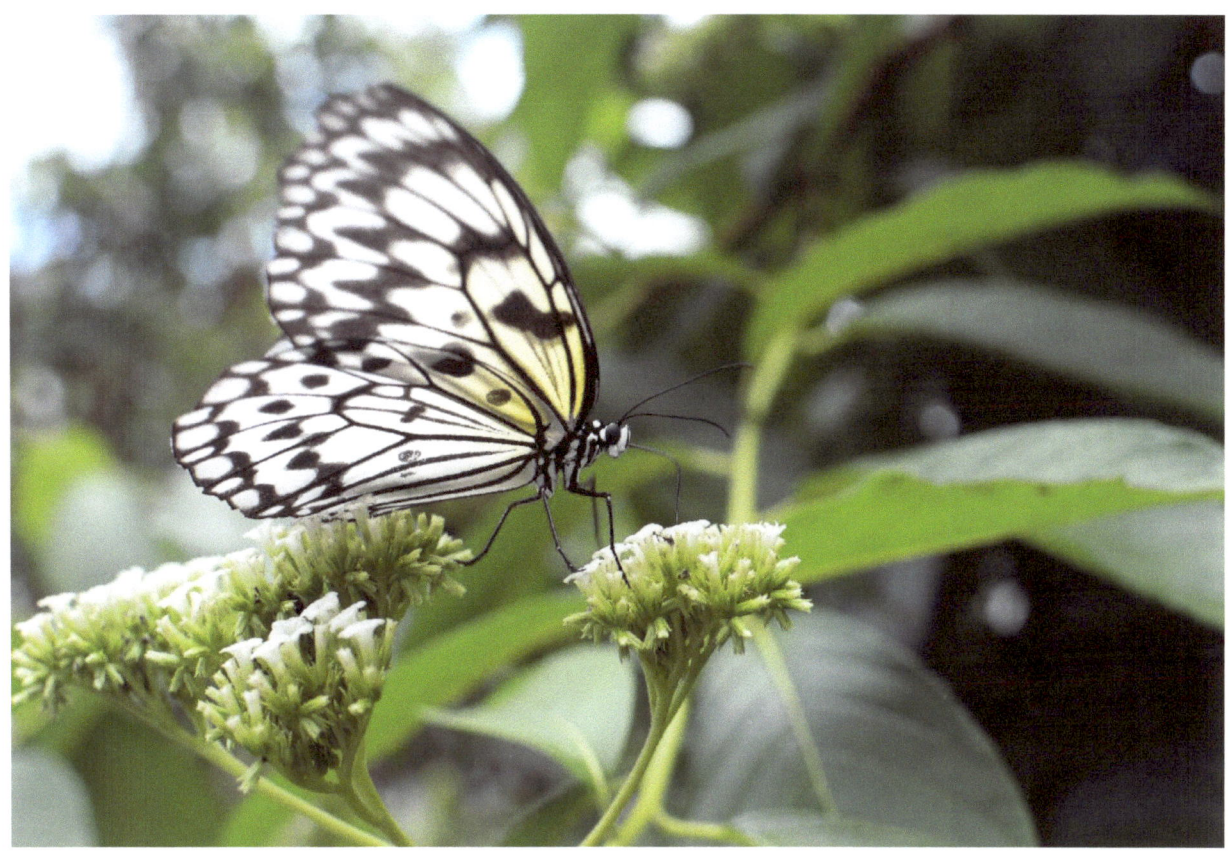

"*A Quick Pit Stop*" Rice Paper

Each one intricately designed

to fascinate!

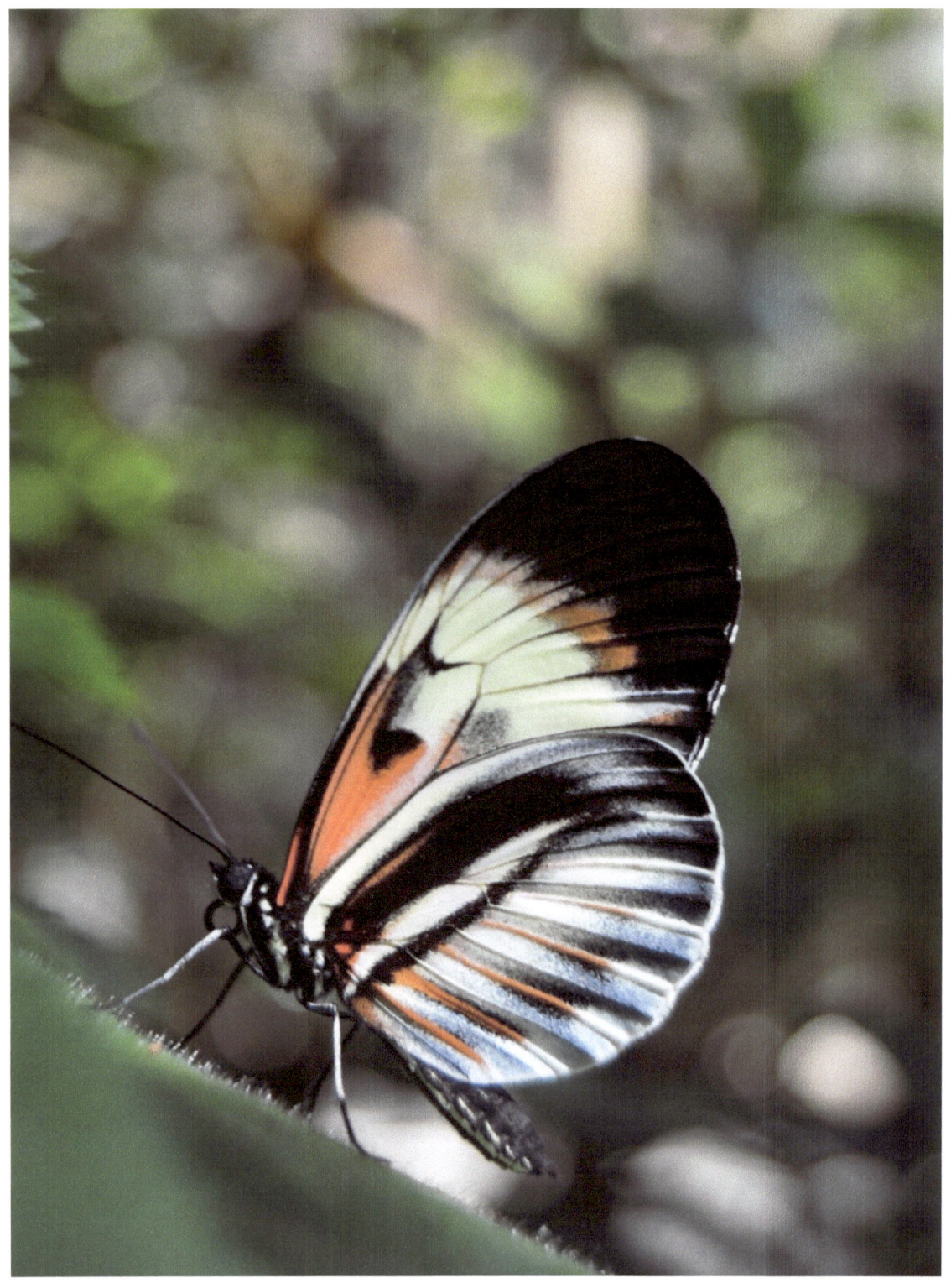

"Bringing Joy"   Postman

The End

About the Author

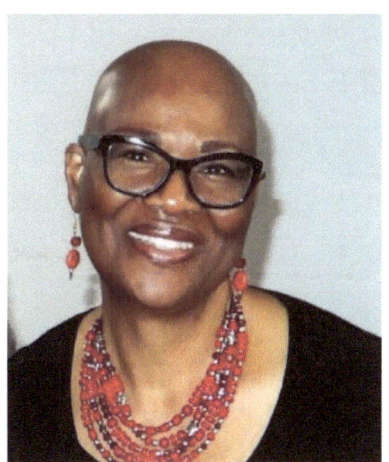

Harriet B. Harris is an Atlanta native who considers herself an "inspirational photographer" for more than 25 years. Her motto is: "Always be camera ready for your vision". She enjoys nature photography, (butterflies in particular), but also animals of all kinds. She occasionally enjoys capturing images of people, particularly her three granddaughters. Her work is not photo-shopped or staged. Her work has been on exhibit numerous times around the Atlanta Metro Area, including at the Hartsfield-Jackson Airport, 2014, when the Monarch butterfly included in this collection was on display. One of her butterfly images also graced the cover of the Dekalb County Public Library Magazine in April 2019. Her next solo exhibit is scheduled for July, 2024, at the Stonecrest Library in Stonecrest, Georgia, when she will again display some of her winged beauties.

She is a mother, grandmother, nurse, certified life coach, and an avid gardener.

This is her second book. Her first book: "*Being Smart About Your Health—A Black Person's Guide to Better Health and a Longer Life in America*", can also be found on her Website, thecircleofsupport.org, on Amazon and Barnes & Nobles. It reflects her passion for health advocacy and the need to be initiative-taking about our health.

For more information on Butterflies, visit sites like the Smithsonian Natural Museum of Natural History: https://naturalhistory.si.edu

Or numerous sites available on Google or YouTube, especially those emphasizing the conservation of these glorious creatures; and how we can participate.

Acknowledgements

To my son, Austin, Daughter-in-law Tyra and my three beautiful granddaughters, Renee', Asha and Tia. You all inspire me to keep capturing beautiful photos which are enjoyed by you and so many others.

To my friend, Pauline Lamar Cooper, you pointed out the need for me to put just a small collection of the numerous photos of butterflies I have captured into a book. Being a great writer yourself, I thank you for pointing out the obvious.

To my friend, Professor Reginal Muhammad. Being a fellow writer also, you encouraged me to finish this project and get it ready for viewing. Your statement: "As a man, I've never paid much attention to butterflies until I saw this"; caused me to realize how impactful this book could become.

To my friend, Felix, whose humor and laughter is always a great inspiration.

REVIEW

In *Listen to the Butterflies,* Ms. Harris puts the outer beauty of these magnificent creatures on display while educating the reader on their inner beauty as well.

Ms. Harris has managed to capture these beautiful butterflies in such a way that you feel as if you are actually viewing them in person. Her photographs of the Monarch and Blue Morpho are my favorite.

She then finds a way to tie the beauty and habits of these small creatures into life lessons from which we can all benefit. The lesson on "Bringing Shameless Beauty Wherever We Go" has become a daily inspiration to me.

Regina Rawls, Academic Adviser, Atlanta Metropolitan College & University